SPANISH FOR LEGAL PRACTITIONERS

Key Terms, Conversations, and Scenarios

Alessio Ruiz

Copyright © 2025 Alessio Ruiz

All rights reserved. No part of this book may be reproduced, or stored in a retrieval system, or transmitted in any form or by any means, electronic, mechanical, photocopying, recording, or otherwise, without express written permission of the publisher.

Trademarks

All terms mentioned in this book that are known to be trademarks or service marks have been appropriately capitalized. The publisher cannot attest to the accuracy of this information. Use of a term in this book should not be regarded as affecting the validity of any trademark or service mark.

Disclaimer

This book is designed to provide information for English speakers seeking to learn Spanish. It is sold with the understanding that the publisher and author are not engaged in rendering legal, financial, medical, or any other professional services. The information contained herein is provided for educational and entertainment purposes only.

While every effort has been made to ensure the reliability and accuracy of the Spanish translations, phrases, and grammatical explanations presented in this work, language is fluid and varies by region. The author and publisher disclaim any responsibility for any errors or omissions, or for the results obtained from the use of this information.

Readers are encouraged to consult with qualified, native-speaking language instructors or reputable sources for confirmation of the material, especially when precise communication is critical.

Limits of Liability

The author and publisher shall have neither liability nor responsibility to any person or entity with respect to any loss or damage caused, or alleged to have been caused, directly or indirectly, by the information contained in this book.

Content Notice

This book is a educational resource. Examples of language may include common slang, idioms, and phrases used in everyday conversation across various Spanish-speaking cultures. These examples are intended for practical learning purposes and do not represent an endorsement of any specific viewpoint.

CONTENTS

Title Page	
Copyright	
Introduction	
How to use this book	1
Initial consultation greetings	3
Dialog	4
Story	5
Scheduling appointments	6
Dialog	7
Story	8
Explaining attorney-client confidentiality	9
Dialog	11
Story	12
Describing legal fees and payment structures	13
Dialog	14
Story	15
Gathering client background information	16
Dialog	17
Story	18
Explaining the legal process	19
Dialog	20

Story	21
Courtroom procedures and etiquette	22
Dialog	23
Story	24
Filing paperwork explanations	25
Dialog	26
Story	27
Document signing procedures	28
Dialog	29
Story	30
Notary public services	31
Dialog	32
Story	33
Divorce proceedings explanation	34
Dialog	36
Story	37
Child custody arrangements	38
Dialog	40
Story	41
Alimony and child support terms	42
Dialog	43
Story	44
Prenuptial agreements	45
Dialog	46
Story	47
Adoption processes	48
Dialog	49
Story	50

Visa application terminology	51
Dialog	52
Story	53
Green card processes	54
Dialog	55
Story	56
Citizenship test preparation	57
Dialog	58
Story	59
Asylum application terms	60
Dialog	61
Story	62
Deportation defense scenarios	63
Dialog	64
Story	65
Arrest rights explanation	66
Dialog	67
Story	68
Bail procedures	69
Dialog	70
Story	71
Plea bargain explanations	72
Dialog	73
Story	74
Probation terms	75
Dialog	76
Story	77
Expungement processes	78

Dialog	79
Story	80
Accident scene descriptions	81
Dialog	82
Story	83
Medical treatment authorization	84
Dialog	85
Story	86
Insurance claim terminology	87
Dialog	88
Story	89
Settlement negotiations	90
Dialog	91
Story	92
Pain and suffering explanations	93
Dialog	94
Story	95
Property purchase contracts	96
Dialog	97
Story	98
Lease agreement explanations	99
Dialog	100
Story	101
Zoning law consultations	102
Dialog	103
Story	104
Eminent domain discussions	105
Dialog	106

Story	107
Title search explanations	108
Dialog	109
Story	110
Wrongful termination terms	111
Dialog	112
Story	113
Workplace discrimination	114
Dialog	115
Story	116
Severance package negotiations	117
Dialog	118
Story	119
Non-compete agreements	120
Dialog	121
Story	122
Workers' compensation claims	123
Dialog	124
Story	125
Will preparation terms	126
Dialog	127
Story	128
Trust fund explanations	129
Dialog	130
Story	131
Power of attorney types	132
Dialog	134
Story	135

Estate tax discussions	136
Dialog	137
Story	138
Inheritance disputes	139
Dialog	140
Story	141
Breach of contract terms	142
Dialog	143
Story	144
Non-disclosure agreements	145
Dialog	146
Story	147
Service contract explanations	148
Dialog	149
Story	150
Termination clauses	151
Dialog	152
Story	153
Liability limitations	154
Dialog	155
Story	156
Bad news delivery phrases	157
Dialog	159
Story	160
Case update terminology	161
Dialog	162
Story	163
Encouraging client patience	164

Dialog	166
Story	167
Requesting documentation	168
Dialog	169
Story	170
Closing a case explanations	171
Dialog	172
Story	173
Addressing the judge	174
Dialog	175
Story	176
Jury instructions	177
Dialog	178
Story	179
Witness examination phrases	180
Dialog	182
Story	183
Objection terminology	184
Dialog	185
Story	186
Closing argument phrases	187
Dialog	188
Story	189
Affidavit explanations	190
Dialog	191
Story	192
Subpoena terminology	193
Dialog	194

Story	195
Deposition procedures	196
Dialog	197
Story	198
Motion filing terms	199
Dialog	200
Story	201
Appeal paperwork vocabulary	202
Dialog	203
Story	204

INTRODUCTION

The legal profession is built on the power of communication. Every case, every client relationship, and every courtroom argument hinges on the precise and effective exchange of information. For the modern lawyer, the ability to bridge linguistic and cultural divides is often a critical professional competency. This book is designed for legal professionals who recognize that serving a broader client base and navigating the globalized landscape of law requires a practical command of the Spanish language.

Traditional language guides often fall short for legal practitioners. They may teach you how to order a meal or ask for directions, but they won't provide the specific vocabulary and phrases needed to conduct a client intake, explain attorney-client confidentiality, or discuss fee structures. This resource is different. It is written to address the real-world scenarios you encounter daily. The content is organized around key practice areas and client interactions, ensuring you learn immediately applicable Spanish that builds client trust and facilitates clearer communication.

We focus on equipping you with key terminology, crucial phrases and practical dialogues—that you can adapt and use immediately. Tis book provides context and procedural insights to ensure your communication is not only grammatically correct but also professionally appropriate. Whether you are meeting with a Spanish-speaking client for the first time, corresponding with counsel, or preparing a witness, this book will serve as a tool to enhance your practice, improve client service, and unlock new professional opportunities.

HOW TO USE THIS BOOK

This book is designed for active learning and immediate application. To maximize its benefits, we would recommend a systematic approach.

Begin by engaging with the foundational chapters, such as initial client greetings and consultations, as these provide the core vocabulary used throughout all client interactions before progressing to more specialized topics.

Utilize the three-part learning structure in each chapter by first familiarizing yourself with the key terms and pronunciations in the vocabulary lists, then studying the sample dialogues to see how the language is used in a natural, professional context, and finally reading the narrative summaries to understand the broader flow of a typical legal scenario.

Practice <u>actively</u> by using the dialogues as templates and substituting different words from the vocabulary lists to create new, relevant conversations for your specific practice.

Focus on comprehension and recall by using the phonetic guides to improve your accent while prioritizing being understood over achieving perfection.

Integrate this learning into your daily routine by keeping the book at your desk for a quick review before a meeting or as a reference to look up a crucial term.

INITIAL CONSULTATION GREETINGS

Buenos días - BWEH-nos DEE-as - Good morning
Buenas tardes - BWEH-nas TAR-des - Good afternoon
Mucho gusto - MOO-cho GOOS-toh - Nice to meet you
Tome asiento - TOH-meh ah-SYEN-toh - Have a seat
¿En qué puedo ayudarle? - en keh PWEH-doh ah-yoo-DAR-leh - How can I help you?
Cuénteme sobre su caso - KWEN-teh-meh SO-breh soo KAH-so - Tell me about your case
Soy el abogado - soy el ah-boh-GAH-doh - I am the lawyer
Soy la abogada - soy lah ah-boh-GAH-dah - I am the lawyer (f)
Bienvenido - byen-veh-NEE-doh - Welcome
Gracias por venir - GRAH-syahs por veh-NEER - Thank you for coming
¿Cómo se siente? - KOH-mo seh SYEN-teh - How are you feeling?
Le explico el proceso - leh eks-PLEE-koh el pro-SE-so - I will explain the process to you
Hablemos de los hechos - ah-BLEH-mos deh los EK-tos - Let's talk about the facts
Todo es confidencial - TOH-doh es kon-fee-den-SYAL - Everything is confidential
¿Tiene alguna pregunta? - TYEH-neh ahl-GOO-nah pre-GOON-tah - Do you have any questions?

DIALOG

Buenos días, tome asiento por favor. ¿En qué puedo ayudarle hoy?

Buenos días. Necesito ayuda con un contrato de arrendamiento que tengo un problema.

Claro, puedo ayudarle con eso. ¿Trajo una copia del contrato para revisar?

Sí, aquí tengo el documento. Muchas gracias.

English translation:
Good morning, please have a seat. How can I help you today?
Good morning. I need help with a rental contract that I have a problem with.
Of course, I can help you with that. Did you bring a copy of the contract to review?
Yes, I have the document here. Thank you very much.

STORY

El abogado recibe al cliente en su despacho. Intercambian saludos y se presentan. El abogado explica el proceso de la consulta inicial y el deber de confidencialidad. El cliente expone brevemente los hechos de su caso. El abogado solicita la documentación relevante para evaluar los antecedentes y determinar la viabilidad legal de una posible demanda.

English translation: The lawyer receives the client in his office. They exchange greetings and introduce themselves. The lawyer explains the initial consultation process and the duty of confidentiality. The client briefly outlines the facts of their case. The lawyer requests relevant documentation to evaluate the background and determine the legal viability of a potential lawsuit.

SCHEDULING APPOINTMENTS

Disponibilidad - dees-poh-nee-bee-lee-DAHD - Availability
Cita - SEE-tah - Appointment
Agenda - ah-HEN-dah - Schedule
Confirmación - kohn-feer-mah-see-OHN - Confirmation
Cancelación - kahn-seh-lah-see-OHN - Cancellation
Abogado/a - ah-boh-GAH-doh/dah - Lawyer
Cliente - klee-EN-teh - Client
Reunión - reh-oo-NYOHN - Meeting
Consulta - kohn-SOOL-tah - Consultation
Oficina - oh-fee-SEE-nah - Office
Fecha - FEH-chah - Date
Hora - OH-rah - Time
Duración - doo-rah-see-OHN - Duration
Asunto - ah-SOON-toh - Matter
Testigo - tehs-TEE-goh - Witness

DIALOG

¿Podría agendar una cita para consultar sobre un contrato de arrendamiento?
Claro, ¿prefiere que sea presencial o virtual?
Presencial, por favor. ¿Tienen disponibilidad este jueves?
Sí, a las diez de la mañana. Necesitaré su número de identificación para confirmar.

English translation:
Could I schedule an appointment to consult about a lease agreement?
Of course, do you prefer it to be in-person or virtual?
In-person, please. Do you have availability this Thursday?
Yes, at ten in the morning. I will need your identification number to confirm.

STORY

El abogado consulta su agenda electrónica. Fija una cita para la audiencia preliminar con el cliente y el procurador. Confirma la fecha y hora para la presentación de escritos. Envía una notificación formal a la contraparte mediante burofax. Todos los involucrados reciben la citación con acuse de recibo para garantizar la validez del procedimiento.

English translation: The lawyer checks his electronic calendar. He sets an appointment for the preliminary hearing with the client and the solicitor. He confirms the date and time for the filing of briefs. He sends a formal notification to the opposing party via certified mail. All involved parties receive the summons with acknowledgment of receipt to guarantee the validity of the procedure.

EXPLAINING ATTORNEY-CLIENT CONFIDENTIALITY

Confidencialidad - kohn-fee-den-syah-lee-DAHD - Confidentiality

Secreto profesional - seh-KREH-toh pro-feh-syo-NAHL - Professional secrecy

Privilegio abogado-cliente - pree-bee-LEH-hyo ah-bo-GAH-doh klee-EN-teh - Attorney-client privilege

Comunicación confidencial - koh-moo-nee-kah-SYON kohn-fee-den-syahL - Confidential communication

Información privilegiada - een-for-mah-SYON pree-bee-leh-HYA-dah - Privileged information

Deber de confidencialidad - DEH-ber deh kohn-fee-den-syah-lee-DAHD - Duty of confidentiality

Relación abogado-cliente - reh-lah-SYON ah-bo-GAH-doh klee-EN-teh - Attorney-client relationship

No divulgación - no dee-vool-gah-SYON - Non-disclosure

Ética profesional - EH-tee-kah pro-feh-syo-NAHL - Professional ethics

Confianza - kohn-FYAN-sah - Trust

Protección legal - proh-tek-SYON leh-GAHL - Legal protection

Revelación indebida - reh-veh-lah-SYON een-deh-BEE-dah - Improper disclosure

Confidencia - kohn-fee-DEN-syah - Confidence

Obligación de secreto - oh-blee-gah-SYON deh seh-KREH-toh - Obligation of secrecy

Derecho a la privacidad - deh-REH-choh ah lah pree-bah-see-DAHD - Right to privacy

DIALOG

¿Puede alguien más, como mi familia, ver lo que hablamos?
No, todo lo que me cuenta es confidencial bajo el secreto profesional.
¿Eso significa que ni siquiera un juez puede obligarle a decirlo?
Exactamente, estoy obligado a guardar el secreto. Sin su permiso, no revelo nada.

English translation:
Can anyone else, like my family, see what we talk about?
No, everything you tell me is confidential under attorney-client privilege.
Does that mean that not even a judge can force you to say it?
Exactly, I am obligated to maintain the secret. Without your permission, I reveal nothing.

STORY

Un abogado recibe información confidencial de su cliente sobre un caso. El abogado no puede divulgar estos hechos a terceros sin el consentimiento expreso del cliente. Este principio, el secreto profesional, es fundamental para la relación abogado-cliente. Permite una defensa efectiva y garantiza que el cliente pueda ser completamente honesto con su representante legal sin temor a revelaciones.

English translation: A lawyer receives confidential information from his client about a case. The lawyer cannot disclose these facts to third parties without the client's express consent. This principle, attorney-client privilege, is fundamental to the lawyer-client relationship. It allows for an effective defense and ensures the client can be completely honest with their legal representative without fear of disclosure.

DESCRIBING LEGAL FEES AND PAYMENT STRUCTURES

Honorarios - oh-noh-rah-REE-ohs - Fees
Pago único - PAH-goh OO-nee-koh - Lump sum payment
Pago por horas - PAH-goh pohr OH-rahs - Hourly rate
Anticipo - ahn-tee-SEE-poh - Retainer
Gastos - GAHS-tohs - Expenses
Factura - fahk-TOO-rah - Invoice
Contingencia - kohn-teen-HEN-see-ah - Contingency
Tarifa plana - tah-REE-fah PLAH-nah - Flat fee
Costas judiciales - KOHS-tahs hoo-dee-see-AH-lehs - Court costs
Honorarios de éxito - oh-noh-rah-REE-ohs deh ek-SEE-toh - Success fee
Pago a plazos - PAH-goh ah PLAH-sohs - Payment in installments
Honorarios fijos - oh-noh-rah-REE-ohs FEE-hohs - Fixed fees
Gastos de representación - GAHS-tohs deh reh-preh-sehn-tah-see-OHN - Representation expenses
Minuta de honorarios - mee-NOO-tah deh oh-noh-rah-REE-ohs - Fee statement
Honorarios razonables - oh-noh-rah-REE-ohs rah-soh-NAH-blehs - Reasonable fees

DIALOG

¿Podría explicarme cómo estructuran sus honorarios legales?
Trabajamos con una tarifa por hora, pero para casos más grandes podemos considerar un precio fijo.
¿Hay algún pago inicial requerido?
Sí, requerimos un anticipo que se deduce del total al final del caso.

English translation:
Could you explain how you structure your legal fees?
We work with an hourly rate, but for larger cases we can consider a fixed price.
Is there an initial payment required?
Yes, we require a retainer that is deducted from the total at the end of the case.

STORY

Los honorarios legales pueden estructurarse de varias formas. Los abogados pueden cobrar una tarifa por hora, un arancel fijo por servicio o un contingente basado en el resultado del caso. Los acuerdos de pago, incluidos los anticipos y los planes de cuotas, deben detallarse por escrito en el contrato de prestación de servicios profesionales para garantizar la transparencia.

English translation: Legal fees can be structured in various ways. Lawyers may charge an hourly rate, a fixed fee per service, or a contingency based on the case outcome. Payment arrangements, including retainers and installment plans, must be detailed in writing in the professional services contract to ensure transparency.

GATHERING CLIENT BACKGROUND INFORMATION

Nombre completo - NOHM-breh kohm-PLEH-toh - Full name
Fecha de nacimiento - FEH-chah deh nah-see-mee-EN-toh - Date of birth
Lugar de nacimiento - loo-GAHR deh nah-see-mee-EN-toh - Place of birth
Nacionalidad - nah-see-oh-nah-lee-DAHD - Nationality
Estado civil - ehs-TAH-doh see-VEEL - Marital status
Profesión - proh-feh-see-ON - Profession
Domicilio - doh-mee-SEE-lee-oh - Address
Número de teléfono - NOO-meh-roh deh teh-LEH-foh-noh - Phone number
Correo electrónico - koh-RREH-oh eh-lek-TROH-nee-koh - Email address
Número de identificación - NOO-meh-roh deh ee-den-tee-fee-kah-see-ON - Identification number
Motivo de la consulta - moh-TEE-voh deh lah kohn-SOOL-tah - Reason for consultation
Hechos relevantes - EH-chohs reh-leh-VAHN-tehs - Relevant facts
Testigos - tehs-TEE-gohs - Witnesses
Pruebas disponibles - PRWEH-bahs dee-spohn-ee-BLEHS - Available evidence
Antecedentes penales - ahn-teh-seh-DEN-tehs peh-NAH-lehs - Criminal record

DIALOG

¿Podría proporcionarme su nombre completo y número de identificación?
Claro, mi nombre es Elena Vargas y mi DNI es X-12345678-A.
¿Necesita que facilite también mi domicilio actual?
Sí, por favor. Y su número de teléfono para contactarla.

English translation:
Could you provide me with your full name and identification number?
Of course, my name is Elena Vargas and my ID number is X-12345678-A.
Do you need me to provide my current address as well?
Yes, please. And your phone number to contact you.

STORY

El abogado revisó los documentos de identificación del cliente y el título de propiedad. Confirmó el estado civil, los nombres de los herederos forzosos y la existencia de testamento previo. Recabó información sobre bienes inmuebles y deudas pendientes. Se programó una nueva cita para la firma de la escritura de donación ante notario.

English translation: The lawyer reviewed the client's identification documents and the property title. He confirmed the marital status, the names of the compulsory heirs, and the existence of a previous will. He gathered information on real estate assets and outstanding debts. A new appointment was scheduled for the signing of the deed of gift before a notary.

EXPLAINING THE LEGAL PROCESS

Demanda - deh-MAN-dah - Lawsuit
Demandado - deh-man-DAH-doh - Defendant
Demandante - deh-man-DAN-teh - Plaintiff
Juez - hoo-ETH - Judge
Abogado - ah-boh-GAH-doh - Lawyer
Testigo - tes-TEE-goh - Witness
Prueba - PRWEH-bah - Evidence
Declaración - deh-klah-rah-see-ON - Statement
Audiencia - ow-dee-EN-see-ah - Hearing
Juicio - HOO-ee-see-oh - Trial
Sentencia - sen-TEN-see-ah - Sentence/Judgment
Acusación - ah-koo-sah-see-ON - Accusation/Charge
Fallo - FAH-yoh - Verdict/Ruling
Prisión preventiva - pree-see-ON preh-ven-TEE-vah - Pre-trial detention
Recurso - reh-KOOR-soh - Appeal/Legal remedy

DIALOG

Primero, se presenta la demanda ante el juzgado competente.
Luego, el demandado es notificado para que presente su respuesta.
¿Y qué pasa si no responde el demandado?
En ese caso, se puede declarar la rebeldía y el proceso continúa.

English translation:
First, the lawsuit is filed with the competent court.
Then, the defendant is notified so they can present their response.
And what happens if the defendant doesn't respond?
In that case, they can be declared in default and the process continues.

STORY

Un cliente presenta una demanda ante el tribunal. El demandado recibe la notificación y presenta su contestación. Ambas partes realizan el descubrimiento de pruebas. Si no hay un acuerdo, el caso procede a juicio. Un juez o jurado emite un veredicto. La parte perdedora puede apelar la sentencia ante un tribunal superior.

English translation: A client files a lawsuit with the court. The defendant receives the notification and files their answer. Both parties conduct discovery of evidence. If there is no settlement, the case proceeds to trial. A judge or jury issues a verdict. The losing party can appeal the judgment to a higher court.

COURTROOM PROCEDURES AND ETIQUETTE

Juez - hoo-ETH - Judge
Abogado - ah-boh-GAH-doh - Lawyer
Testigo - tes-TEE-goh - Witness
Declaración - deh-klah-rah-see-ON - Testimony
Juramento - hoo-rah-MEN-toh - Oath
Prueba - PRWEH-bah - Evidence
Declararse culpable - deh-klah-RAHR-seh kool-PAH-bleh - To plead guilty
Declararse inocente - deh-klah-RAHR-seh ee-noh-SEN-teh - To plead not guilty
Veredicto - veh-reh-DEEK-toh - Verdict
Sentencia - sen-TEN-see-ah - Sentence
Tribunal - tree-boo-NAHL - Court
Fiscal - fees-KAHL - Prosecutor
Acusado - ah-koo-SAH-doh - Defendant
Silencio - see-LEN-see-oh - Silence
Poder judicial - poh-DER hoo-dee-see-AHL - Judiciary

DIALOG

Señoría, solicito permiso para acercarme al testigo.
Concedido. Puede proceder con su interrogatorio.
¿Podría decirnos qué vio la noche del incidente?
Objectión. La pregunta induce al testigo.

STORY

El juez declaró abierta la sesión. El abogado presentó una objeción, pero la parte contraria la refutó. El testigo prestó juramento y declaró. El fiscal interpuso un recurso y presentó pruebas documentales. El tribunal admitió las pruebas y las agregó al expediente. El juez escuchó los argumentos finales y emitió su veredicto basado en la ley.

English translation: The judge declared the session open. The lawyer presented an objection, but the opposing party refuted it. The witness took the oath and testified. The prosecutor filed an appeal and presented documentary evidence. The court admitted the evidence and added it to the case file. The judge heard the final arguments and issued his verdict based on the law.

FILING PAPERWORK EXPLANATIONS

Poder - poh-DEHR - Power of Attorney
Escritura - es-kree-TOO-rah - Deed
Contrato - kon-TRAH-toh - Contract
Demanda - deh-MAN-dah - Lawsuit
Testamento - tes-tah-MEN-toh - Will
Declaración Jurada - deh-klah-rah-see-ON hoo-RAH-dah - Sworn Statement
Sello - SEH-yoh - Stamp
Firma - FEER-mah - Signature
Juramento - hoo-rah-MEN-toh - Oath
Notario - noh-TAH-ree-oh - Notary Public
Certificado - sehr-tee-fee-KAH-doh - Certificate
Registro - reh-HEES-troh - Registry
Expediente - eks-peh-dee-EN-teh - File / Case File
Anexo - ah-NEK-soh - Attachment
Comparecencia - kom-pah-reh-SEN-see-ah - Appearance (in court)

DIALOG

¿Tiene todos los documentos necesarios para la solicitud?
Sí, aquí están el formulario notarizado y los anexos requeridos.
Perfecto. Solo falta que firme aquí, al pie de la última página.
Claro, ¿debo fecharlo también con la fecha de hoy?

STORY

El abogado presentó la demanda ante el tribunal. Adjuntó los anexos requeridos y las pruebas pertinentes. La secretaria judicial le otorgó un sello de recepción con la fecha y el número de expediente. Este comprobante acredita la presentación formal dentro del plazo legal establecido para dichos actos procesales.

English translation: The lawyer filed the lawsuit before the court. He attached the required exhibits and pertinent evidence. The court clerk provided a receipt stamp with the date and case number. This voucher certifies the formal filing within the legal deadline established for such procedural actions.

DOCUMENT SIGNING PROCEDURES

Firma - FEER-mah - Signature
Firmante - feer-MAHN-teh - Signatory
Testigo - tehs-TEE-goh - Witness
Notario - noh-TAH-ree-oh - Notary Public
Documento - doh-koo-MEN-toh - Document
Copia Fiel - KOH-peeah fee-EL - Certified Copy
Sello - SEH-yoh - Seal
Acta - AHK-tah - Deed / Minutes
Protocolo - proh-toh-KOH-loh - Notarial Protocol
Autenticación - ow-ten-tee-kah-see-ON - Authentication
Legalización - leh-gah-lee-sah-see-ON - Legalization
Poder - poh-DEHR - Power of Attorney
Otorgante - oh-tohr-GAHN-teh - Grantor
Beneficiario - beh-neh-fee-see-AH-ree-oh - Beneficiary
Juramento - hoo-rah-MEN-toh - Oath

DIALOG

¿Está listo para proceder con la firma de los documentos?
Sí, he revisado todas las cláusulas y estoy de acuerdo.
Perfecto. Firme aquí, al pie de la página, por favor.
Hecho. Aquí tiene su copia del contrato firmado.

English translation:
Are you ready to proceed with signing the documents?
Yes, I have reviewed all the clauses and I agree.
Perfect. Please sign here, at the bottom of the page.
Done. Here is your copy of the signed contract.

STORY

El notario verificó la identidad de los comparecientes y la capacidad jurídica. Leyó íntegramente la escritura pública para asegurar la comprensión. Las partes manifestaron su conformidad y procedieron a firmar el documento. El notario rubricó todas las páginas y estampó su sello, otorgando fe pública al acto. Finalmente, se instruyó sobre el procedimiento de inscripción en el registro correspondiente.

English translation: The notary verified the identity of the appearing parties and their legal capacity. He read the public deed in its entirety to ensure understanding. The parties stated their agreement and proceeded to sign the document. The notary signed every page and stamped his seal, granting public faith to the act. Finally, instructions were given on the procedure for registration in the corresponding registry.

NOTARY PUBLIC SERVICES

Notario Público - noh-TAH-ree-oh POO-blee-koh - Notary Public
Acta Notarial - AHK-tah noh-tah-REE-ahl - Notarial Act
Fe Pública - feh POO-blee-kah - Public Faith
Protocolo - proh-toh-KOH-loh - Notarial Protocol
Testigo - tehs-TEE-goh - Witness
Identificación - ee-den-tee-fee-kah-see-OHN - Identification
Comparecencia - kohm-pah-reh-SEN-see-ah - Appearance
Juramento - hoo-rah-MEN-toh - Oath
Firma - FEER-mah - Signature
Sello Notarial - SEH-yoh noh-tah-REE-ahl - Notarial Seal
Legalización - leh-gah-lee-sah-see-OHN - Authentication
Poder Notarial - poh-DEHR noh-tah-REE-ahl - Power of Attorney
Escritura Pública - es-kree-TOO-rah POO-blee-kah - Public Deed
Fe de Hechos - feh deh EH-chohs - Certification of Facts
Apostilla - ah-pohs-TEE-yah - Apostille

DIALOG

¿Tiene usted los documentos de identificación necesarios para la firma?

Sí, aquí tiene mi pasaporte vigente y el documento de la propiedad.

Perfecto. Procederemos a la lectura íntegra del acta notarial.

De acuerdo, procedamos con la lectura para luego firmar.

English translation:

Do you have the necessary identification documents for the signing?

Yes, here is my valid passport and the property deed.

Perfect. We will proceed with the complete reading of the notarial deed.

Agreed, let us proceed with the reading and then sign.

STORY

El notario certificó la escritura pública de compraventa. Las partes comparecieron con sus documentos de identidad. El notario verificó su capacidad jurídica y la legalidad del contrato. Leyó el instrumento en voz alta y las partes lo firmaron. Luego, el notario estampó su firma y sello, otorgándole fe pública al documento.

English translation: The notary certified the public deed of sale. The parties appeared with their identification documents. The notary verified their legal capacity and the contract's legality. He read the instrument aloud and the parties signed it. Then, the notary affixed his signature and seal, granting public faith to the document.

DIVORCE PROCEEDINGS EXPLANATION

Demanda de divorcio - deh-MAN-dah deh dee-VOR-syo - Divorce petition
Sentencia de divorcio - sen-TEN-syah deh dee-VOR-syo - Divorce decree
Separación legal - seh-pah-rah-SYON leh-GAHL - Legal separation
Cónyuge - KON-yoo-heh - Spouse
Pensión alimenticia - pen-SYON ah-lee-men-TEE-syah - Alimony / Child support
Custodia - koos-TOH-dyah - Custody
Patria potestad - PAH-tryah poh-tes-TAHD - Parental rights and responsibilities
Divorcio contencioso - dee-VOR-syo kon-ten-SYO-so - Contested divorce
Divorcio de mutuo acuerdo - dee-VOR-syo deh MOO-too-oh ah-KWER-doh - Uncontested divorce / Divorce by mutual agreement
Liquidación de bienes - lee-kee-dah-SYON deh BYEH-nes - Division of assets
Acuerdo prenupcial - ah-KWER-doh preh-noop-SYAHL - Prenuptial agreement
Mediación - meh-dyah-SYON - Mediation
Juez - hoo-ETH - Judge
Abogado - ah-boh-GAH-doh - Lawyer

Prueba - PRWEH-bah - Evidence

DIALOG

¿Podría explicar el proceso de divorcio de mutuo acuerdo?
Claro. Primero, presentamos la demanda junto con el convenio regulador.
¿Y qué debe incluir ese convenio?
Debe detallar la custodia, la pensión alimenticia y la división de bienes.

English translation:
Could you explain the process for a mutual agreement divorce?
Of course. First, we file the petition along with the settlement agreement.
And what should that agreement include?
It must detail custody, alimony, and the division of assets.

STORY

La demandante presenta una demanda de divorcio de mutuo acuerdo. Ambos cónyuges han firmado un convenio regulador que detalla la pensión alimenticia y la custodia compartida de los hijos menores. Solicitan la disolución del vínculo matrimonial conforme a la ley. El juez, revisando la documentación, procede a dictar la sentencia.

English translation: The plaintiff files a petition for divorce by mutual agreement. Both spouses have signed a settlement agreement detailing child support and shared custody of the minor children. They request the dissolution of the marriage according to the law. The judge, reviewing the documentation, proceeds to issue the ruling.

CHILD CUSTODY ARRANGEMENTS

Custodia - koo-STOH-dee-ah - Custody
Patria Potestad - PAH-tree-ah poh-teh-STAD - Parental Rights and Responsibilities
Guarda y Custodia - GWAR-dah ee koo-STOH-dee-ah - Guardianship and Custody
Custodia Compartida - koo-STOH-dee-ah kohm-par-TEE-dah - Joint Custody
Custodia Exclusiva - koo-STOH-dee-ah ek-sklu-SEE-vah - Sole Custody
Régimen de Visitas - REH-hee-men deh vee-SEE-tas - Visitation Schedule
Pensión de Alimentos - pen-SYOHN deh ah-lee-MEN-tohs - Child Support
Convenio Regulador - kohn-VEH-nyoh reh-goo-lah-DOR - Settlement Agreement
Derecho de Visita - deh-REH-choh deh vee-SEE-tah - Right of Visitation
Interés Superior del Menor - in-teh-RES soo-peh-ree-OR del meh-NOR - Best Interest of the Child
Domicilio Conyugal - doh-mee-SEE-lyoh kohn-yoo-GAHL - Marital Home
Mediación Familiar - meh-dee-ah-SYOHN fah-mee-lee-AR - Family Mediation
Oído del Menor - oh-EE-doh del meh-NOR - Heard the Child (Child's Testimony)
Punto de Encuentro - POON-toh deh en-KWEN-troh - Meeting

Point (Neutral Exchange Location)
Auto - OW-toh - Court Order

DIALOG

¿Cuándo podré ver a los niños?
Según el acuerdo, tienes derecho a visitas los fines de semana alternos.
¿Y qué pasa con las vacaciones de verano?
El período de vacaciones se dividirá en dos partes iguales.

English translation:
When will I be able to see the children?
According to the agreement, you have the right to visitation on alternating weekends.
And what about summer vacation?
The vacation period will be divided into two equal parts.

STORY

El juez emitió la sentencia de custodia. Otorgó la custodia compartida a ambos progenitores. El convenio regulador establece el régimen de visitas y la pensión alimenticia. Los hijos permanecerán con la madre durante la semana. El padre tendrá su guarda los fines de semana alternos. Ambos tutores legales deben cumplir el acuerdo. La sentencia es firme y ejecutable.

English translation: The judge issued the custody ruling. He granted shared custody to both parents. The settlement agreement establishes the visitation schedule and child support. The children will remain with the mother during the week. The father will have his custody on alternate weekends. Both legal guardians must comply with the agreement. The ruling is final and enforceable.

ALIMONY AND CHILD SUPPORT TERMS

Pensión alimenticia - pen-SYON ah-lee-MEN-tee-syah - Alimony
Manutención de menores - mah-noo-ten-SYON deh meh-NO-res - Child support
Obligación alimentaria - oh-blee-gah-SYON ah-lee-men-TAH-ryah - Support obligation
Pensión para los hijos - pen-SYON PAH-rah los EE-hos - Child support payment
Cuota alimentaria - KWAH-tah ah-lee-men-TAH-ryah - Support allowance
Cónyuge - KON-yoo-heh - Spouse
Acuerdo - ah-KWER-doh - Agreement
Convenio regulador - kon-VEN-yo reh-goo-lah-DOR - Settlement agreement
Demanda - deh-MAN-dah - Petition / Lawsuit
Juzgado de familia - hoo-GAH-doh deh fah-MEE-lyah - Family court
Juez - hoo-ETH - Judge
Sentencia - sen-TEN-syah - Judgment / Sentence
Ejecución - eh-heh-koo-SYON - Enforcement
Embargo de bienes - em-BAR-goh deh BYEN-es - Garnishment of assets
Atrasos - ah-TRAH-sos - Arrears

DIALOG

¿Está de acuerdo con el monto de la pensión alimenticia propuesto?
Sí, pero necesito que se incluya un ajuste anual por inflación.
También debemos especificar los gastos extraordinarios para los niños.
De acuerdo. Incluiremos ambos términos en el convenio.

English translation:
Do you agree with the proposed alimony amount?
Yes, but I need an annual adjustment for inflation to be included.
We must also specify the extraordinary expenses for the children.
Agreed. We will include both terms in the agreement.

STORY

El demandante solicitó la pensión alimenticia y la custodia ante el tribunal. El juez fijó una cuantía mensual para la manutención de los hijos menores. La sentencia establece la obligación de pago hasta la mayoría de edad. El convenio regulador incluye la pensión compensatoria y el régimen de visitas.

English translation: The petitioner requested alimony and custody before the court. The judge set a monthly amount for the child support. The ruling establishes the payment obligation until the age of majority. The settlement agreement includes compensatory alimony and visitation rights.

PRENUPTIAL AGREEMENTS

Pacto Antenupcial - PAHK-toh ahn-teh-noop-see-AHL - Prenuptial Agreement

Capitulaciones Matrimoniales - kah-pee-too-lah-see-OH-nes mah-tree-moh-nee-AH-les - Matrimonial Agreements

Régimen Económico Matrimonial - REH-hee-men eh-koh-NOH-mee-koh mah-tree-moh-NYAHL - Matrimonial Property Regime

Separación de Bienes - seh-pah-rah-see-ON deh bee-EN-es - Separation of Property

Sociedad de Gananciales - soh-see-eh-DAHD deh gah-nahn-see-AH-les - Community Property

Bienes Propios - bee-EN-es PROH-pee-os - Separate Property

Bienes Gananciales - bee-EN-es gah-nahn-see-AH-les - Marital Property

Deudas - DEH-oo-dahs - Debts

Liquidación - lee-kee-dah-see-ON - Liquidation

Cláusula - KLAH-oo-soo-lah - Clause

Disolución Matrimonial - dee-soh-loo-see-ON mah-tree-moh-NYAHL - Dissolution of Marriage

Nulidad - noo-lee-DAHD - Annulment

Herencia - eh-REN-see-ah - Inheritance

Donación - doh-nah-see-ON - Gift/Donation

Renuncia - reh-NOON-see-ah - Waiver

DIALOG

¿Está listo para revisar las cláusulas patrimoniales del convenio?
Sí, pero debemos especificar qué bienes se consideran propios.
De acuerdo. También debemos incluir una cláusula de liquidación.
Perfecto. Así quedan protegidos los derechos de ambos.

English translation:
Are you ready to review the asset clauses of the agreement?
Yes, but we must specify which assets are considered separate property.
Agreed. We must also include a liquidation clause.
Perfect. This way the rights of both parties are protected.

STORY

Antes de la boda, los futuros cónyuges firmaron un acuerdo prenupcial. El contrato, redactado por un abogado, especificaba el régimen económico matrimonial de separación de bienes. Ambos declararon sus patrimonios iniciales. El notario autorizó la escritura pública, cumpliendo con todos los requisitos legales. El acuerdo determinó la liquidación de la sociedad de gananciales tras el divorcio.

English translation: Before the wedding, the future spouses signed a prenuptial agreement. The contract, drafted by a lawyer, specified the marital economic regime of separation of property. Both declared their initial assets. The notary authorized the public deed, complying with all legal requirements. The agreement determined the liquidation of the community property after the divorce.

ADOPTION PROCESSES

Adopción - ah-dohp-see-OHN - Adoption
Adoptante - ah-dohp-TAHN-teh - Adoptive parent
Adoptado - ah-dohp-TAH-doh - Adopted child
Consentimiento - kohn-sen-tee-mee-EHN-toh - Consent
Patria Potestad - PAH-tree-ah poh-tehs-TAHD - Parental rights and responsibilities
Idoneidad - ee-doh-nay-DAHD - Suitability / Fitness
Juicio de Adopción - HOO-ee-see-oh deh ah-dohp-see-OHN - Adoption proceeding
Informe Psicosocial - een-FOR-meh see-koh-soh-see-AHL - Psychosocial report
Orfandad - ohr-fahn-DAHD - Orphanhood
Tutela - too-TEH-lah - Guardianship
Juez de Familia - HOO-ehz deh fah-MEE-lee-ah - Family Court Judge
Registro Civil - reh-HEES-troh see-VEEL - Civil Registry
Acta de Adopción - AHK-tah deh ah-dohp-see-OHN - Adoption certificate
Proceso Legal - proh-SEH-soh leh-GAHL - Legal process
Conformidad - kohn-for-mee-DAHD - Agreement / Conformity

DIALOG

¿Ha presentado ya la solicitud de idoneidad para la adopción?
Sí, y el equipo técnico ya emitió su informe favorable.
Perfecto. Ahora debemos esperar la propuesta de asignación del menor.
De acuerdo. Estaremos atentos a la notificación de la resolución judicial.

English translation:
Have you already submitted the suitability application for adoption?
Yes, and the technical team has already issued their favorable report.
Perfect. Now we must wait for the child assignment proposal.
Agreed. We will be attentive to the notification of the judicial resolution.

STORY

La pareja presentó la solicitud de adopción ante el Juzgado de Primera Instancia. El equipo técnico emitió su informe psicosocial favorable. El Ministerio Público dio su conformidad. Tras la propuesta previa de la entidad colaboradora, el juez dictó la resolución judicial de adopción, declarando la filiación. Se inscribió la sentencia firme en el Registro Civil.

English translation: The couple filed the adoption application with the Court of First Instance. The technical team issued a favorable psychosocial report. The Public Prosecutor gave its consent. Following the preliminary proposal from the collaborating agency, the judge issued the judicial adoption order, establishing the filiation. The final ruling was registered with the Civil Registry.

VISA APPLICATION TERMINOLOGY

Solicitud de Visa - soh-lee-see-TOOD deh VEE-sah - Visa Application
Formulario - for-moo-LAH-ryoh - Form
Pasaporte - pah-sah-POR-teh - Passport
Fotografía - foh-toh-grah-FEE-ah - Photograph
Huellas Digitales - WEH-yahs dee-hee-TAH-lehs - Fingerprints
Declaración Jurada - deh-klah-rah-see-ON hoo-RAH-dah - Sworn Statement
Documento de Identidad - doh-koo-MEN-toh deh ee-den-tee-DAHD - Identity Document
Estado Civil - ehs-TAH-doh see-VEEL - Marital Status
Antecedentes Penales - ahn-teh-seh-DEN-tehs peh-NAH-lehs - Criminal Record
Residencia Permanente - reh-see-DEN-see-ah pehr-mah-NEN-teh - Permanent Residence
Permiso de Trabajo - pehr-MEE-soh deh trah-BAH-hoh - Work Permit
Patrocinador - pah-troh-see-nah-DOR - Sponsor
Solicitante - soh-lee-see-TAHN-teh - Applicant
Cónyuge - KOHN-yoo-heh - Spouse
Entrevista - en-treh-VEES-tah - Interview

DIALOG

¿Tiene usted un expediente administrativo pendiente?
No, no tengo antecedentes penales ni procesos judiciales abiertos.
¿Presenta usted una carta de invitación para su estancia?
Sí, aquí tiene el documento notarial que acredita mi patrocinio económico.

English translation:
Do you have any pending administrative proceedings?
No, I have no criminal record or open judicial processes.
Are you presenting a letter of invitation for your stay?
Yes, here is the notarized document that proves my financial sponsorship.

STORY

El solicitante presentó su solicitud de visa junto con la documentación de respaldo requerida. La embajada verificó su elegibilidad y estatus migratorio. Tras una revisión exhaustiva, se emitió la visa de residencia permanente. El titular ahora debe cumplir con los términos de su admisión y mantener su estatus legal para evitar la deportación.

English translation: The applicant submitted their visa application along with the required supporting documentation. The embassy verified their eligibility and immigration status. After a thorough review, the permanent residency visa was issued. The holder must now comply with the terms of their admission and maintain their legal status to avoid deportation.

GREEN CARD PROCESSES

Residencia Permanente - reh-see-DEN-see-ah pehr-mah-NEN-teh - Permanent Residence
Tarjeta Verde - tar-HEH-tah BEHR-deh - Green Card
Formulario - for-moo-LAH-ree-oh - Form
Solicitud - soh-lee-see-TOOD - Application
Petición Familiar - peh-tee-see-OHN fah-mee-lee-AHR - Family Petition
Ajuste de Estatus - ah-HOOS-teh deh eh-STAT-oos - Adjustment of Status
Beneficiario - beh-neh-fee-see-AH-ree-oh - Beneficiary
Patrocinador - pah-troh-see-nah-DOR - Sponsor
Declaración Jurada - deh-klah-rah-see-OHN hoo-RAH-dah - Sworn Statement
Entrevista - en-treh-VEES-tah - Interview
Huellas Digitales - WEH-yahs dee-hee-TAH-les - Fingerprints
Permiso de Trabajo - pehr-MEE-soh deh trah-BAH-ho - Work Permit
Notificación de Acción - noh-tee-fee-kah-see-OHN deh ahk-see-OHN - Notice of Action
Causa de Inadmisibilidad - KOW-sah deh een-ahd-mee-see-bee-lee-DAHD - Ground of Inadmissibility
Renovación - reh-noh-bah-see-OHN - Renewal

DIALOG

¿Ya presentó la petición de visa para su cónyuge?
Sí, presenté el Formulario I-130 la semana pasada.
¿Recibió el acuse de recibo del Servicio de Ciudadanía e Inmigración?
Todavía no, estoy esperando la notificación por correo.

English translation:
Have you already filed the visa petition for your spouse?
Yes, I filed the Form I-130 last week.
Did you receive the receipt notice from Citizenship and Immigration Services?
Not yet, I am waiting for the notification by mail.

STORY

El abogado presentó la petición I-130 y el formulario I-485 para ajuste de estatus. Se adjuntaron los affidavit de sostén y la evidencia de elegibilidad. Tras la biometría, se programó la entrevista. El oficial de USCIS revisó la documentación. La residencia permanente fue concedida. Se notificó la aprobación por escrito.

English translation: The lawyer filed the I-130 petition and the I-485 form for adjustment of status. The affidavits of support and evidence of eligibility were attached. After the biometrics, the interview was scheduled. The USCIS officer reviewed the documentation. Permanent residence was granted. The approval was notified in writing.

CITIZENSHIP TEST PREPARATION

Derechos - deh-REH-chos - Rights
Deberes - deh-BEH-res - Duties
Constitución - kohns-tee-too-see-ON - Constitution
Gobierno - goh-bee-ER-noh - Government
Ley - lay - Law
Ciudadanía - see-oo-dah-dah-NEE-ah - Citizenship
Residente permanente - reh-see-DEN-teh per-meh-NEN-teh - Permanent resident
Juramento - hoo-rah-MEN-toh - Oath
Nacionalización - nah-see-oh-nah-lee-sah-see-ON - Naturalization
Votar - voh-TAR - To vote
Impuestos - eem-PWEH-stos - Taxes
Sistema judicial - see-STEH-mah hoo-dee-see-AL - Judicial system
Libertad - lee-behr-TAHD - Freedom
Democracia - deh-moh-KRAH-see-ah - Democracy
Sufragio - soo-FRAH-hee-oh - Suffrage

DIALOG

¿Está listo para prestar juramento a la Constitución?
Sí, juro defender la Constitución y las leyes de los Estados Unidos.
¿Renuncia a su lealtad a su país de origen anterior?
Sí, renuncio a toda lealtad anterior.

English translation:
Are you ready to take the Oath of Allegiance to the Constitution?
Yes, I swear to defend the Constitution and the laws of the United States.
Do you renounce your allegiance to your previous country of origin?
Yes, I renounce all prior allegiance.

STORY

Un ciudadano solicita la nacionalidad española. Presenta su solicitud, documentación y pago de tasas ante el funcionario. La oficina de extranjería registra la petición y emite un recibo. Inicia un procedimiento administrativo. Tras verificar los requisitos de residencia y conducta cívica, el Ministerio de Justicia concede la nacionalidad por resolución. Finalmente, jura la Constitución ante el juez.

English translation: A citizen applies for Spanish nationality. He submits his application, documentation, and payment of fees before the official. The immigration office registers the petition and issues a receipt. An administrative procedure begins. After verifying the requirements of residence and civic conduct, the Ministry of Justice grants nationality by resolution. Finally, he swears to the Constitution before the judge.

ASYLUM APPLICATION TERMS

Asilo - ah-SEE-loh - Asylum
Refugiado - reh-foo-HYAH-doh - Refugee
Solicitud de Asilo - soh-lee-see-TOOD deh ah-SEE-loh - Asylum Application
Temor Fundado - teh-MOR foon-DAH-doh - Well-Founded Fear
Persecución - pehr-seh-koo-SYON - Persecution
Agente de Asilo - ah-HEN-teh deh ah-SEE-loh - Asylum Officer
Audiencia - ow-DYEN-syah - Hearing
Juez de Inmigración - HOO-ez deh eem-mee-grah-SYON - Immigration Judge
Abogado - ah-boh-GAH-doh - Lawyer
Intérprete - een-TEHR-preh-teh - Interpreter
Declaración - deh-klah-rah-SYON - Statement / Testimony
Testigo - tehs-TEE-goh - Witness
Credibilidad - kreh-dee-bee-lee-DAHD - Credibility
Miedo Creíble - MYEH-doh kray-EE-bleh - Credible Fear
Deportación - deh-por-tah-SYON - Deportation

DIALOG

¿Ha presentado su solicitud de asilo en la frontera?
Sí, presenté la solicitud de asilo al ingresar al país.
¿Comprendió los términos de la declaración jurada que firmó?
Sí, entendí que debo decir la verdad en mi testimonio.

English translation:
Have you submitted your asylum application at the border?
Yes, I submitted the asylum application upon entering the country.
Did you understand the terms of the affidavit you signed?
Yes, I understood that I must tell the truth in my testimony.

STORY

El solicitante, nacional de Honduras, llegó a la frontera y expresó su intención de solicitar asilo. Temía la persecución por parte de un grupo criminal en su país de origen. Presentó su declaración jurada y documentación de identidad. Su caso fue remitido para una audiencia de miedo creíble ante un oficial de asilo. Actualmente aguarda la resolución de su petición.

English translation: The applicant, a national of Honduras, arrived at the border and expressed his intention to request asylum. He feared persecution from a criminal group in his country of origin. He presented his sworn affidavit and identification documentation. His case was referred for a credible fear hearing before an asylum officer. He currently awaits the resolution of his petition.

DEPORTATION DEFENSE SCENARIOS

Deportación - deh-por-tah-see-ON - Deportation
Asilo - ah-SEE-loh - Asylum
Cancelación de Remoción - kan-seh-lah-see-ON deh reh-moh-see-ON - Cancellation of Removal
Ajuste de Estatus - ah-HOOS-teh deh eh-STAT-oos - Adjustment of Status
Salvaguardias - sahl-vah-GWAR-dee-ahs - Safeguards
Audiencia - ow-DYEN-see-ah - Hearing
Juez de Inmigración - hoo-EZ deh eem-ee-grah-see-ON - Immigration Judge
Fianza - fee-AN-sah - Bond
Alivio - ah-LEE-vee-oh - Relief
Estatus de Protección Temporal - eh-STAT-oos deh proh-tek-see-ON tem-poh-RAHL - Temporary Protected Status
Aviso de Comparecencia - ah-VEE-soh deh kom-pah-reh-SEN-see-ah - Notice to Appear
Solicitud - soh-lee-see-TOOD - Application / Petition
Apelación - ah-peh-lah-see-ON - Appeal
Salida Voluntaria - sah-LEE-dah voh-loon-TAH-ree-ah - Voluntary Departure
Moción - moh-see-ON - Motion

DIALOG

¿Tiene miedo de regresar a su país de origen?
Sí, mucho miedo. Allá me han amenazado.
¿Quién lo amenazó y por qué motivo?
Mi primo, porque me negué a unirme a su pandilla.

English translation:
Are you afraid to return to your home country?
Yes, very afraid. I have been threatened there.
Who threatened you and for what reason?
My cousin, because I refused to join his gang.

STORY

El cliente fue detenido en una redada. Presentamos un recurso ante la corte de inmigración solicitando asilo. Alegamos temor fundado de persecución en su país de origen. La jueza revisó la evidencia y los testimonios. Concedió la fianza y programó una audiencia futura. El caso continúa en proceso.

English translation: The client was detained in a raid. We filed a motion in immigration court requesting asylum. We alleged a well-founded fear of persecution in his country of origin. The judge reviewed the evidence and testimony. She granted bond and scheduled a future hearing. The case remains ongoing.

ARREST RIGHTS EXPLANATION

Derecho a permanecer callado - deh-REH-choh ah pehr-mah-neh-SEHR kah-YAH-doh - Right to remain silent

Derecho a un abogado - deh-REH-choh ah oon ah-boh-GAH-doh - Right to an attorney

Abogado de oficio - ah-boh-GAH-doh deh oh-FEE-see-oh - Court-appointed lawyer

Entender los cargos - en-ten-DEHR lohs KAHR-gohs - To understand the charges

Declarar - deh-klah-RAHR - To make a statement

Interrogatorio - een-teh-rroh-gah-TOH-ryoh - Interrogation

Custodia - koos-TOH-dyah - Custody

Fianza - fee-AHN-sah - Bail

Juez - hoo-ETH - Judge

Corte - KOR-teh - Court

Cargos - KAHR-gohs - Charges

Acusación - ah-koo-sah-see-OHN - Accusation

Detención - deh-ten-see-OHN - Detention

Averiguación - ah-veh-ree-gwah-see-OHN - Inquiry/Investigation

Proceso legal - proh-SEH-soh leh-GAHL - Legal process

DIALOG

Tiene derecho a guardar silencio. Todo lo que diga puede ser usado en su contra.
¿Entiendo. Tengo derecho a un abogado, verdad?
Sí. Si no tiene recursos, se le designará uno de oficio.
Quiero ejercer ese derecho y hablar con mi abogado ahora.

English translation:
You have the right to remain silent. Anything you say can be used against you.
I understand. I have the right to a lawyer, correct?
Yes. If you do not have the means, one will be appointed to you.
I wish to exercise that right and speak with my lawyer now.

STORY

El agente informó al detenido de sus derechos constitucionales. Le comunicó su derecho a guardar silencio y a designar un abogado. Le notificó que, de no poder pagar uno, se le nombraría un defensor público. El detenido confirmó que comprendía la declaración de derechos antes de cualquier interrogatorio.

English translation: The officer informed the detainee of his constitutional rights. He communicated his right to remain silent and to appoint a lawyer. He notified him that, if he could not pay for one, a public defender would be appointed. The detainee confirmed he understood the Miranda warning before any questioning.

BAIL PROCEDURES

Fianza - fee-AHN-sah - Bail
Libertad bajo fianza - lee-behr-TAHD BAH-ho fee-AHN-sah - Release on bail
Juez - hoo-ETH - Judge
Audiencia - ow-DYEN-syah - Hearing
Monto de la fianza - MOHN-toh deh lah fee-AHN-sah - Bail amount
Fiador - fee-ah-DOR - Bail bondsman / Guarantor
Pagar fianza - pah-GAHR fee-AHN-sah - To post bail
Embargo preventivo - ehm-BAHR-goh preh-vehn-TEE-voh - Freeze order / Preemptive seizure
Fianza excesiva - fee-AHN-sah ek-seh-SEE-sah - Excessive bail
Fianza razonable - fee-AHN-sah rah-soh-NAH-bleh - Reasonable bail
Comparecencia - kohm-pah-reh-SEN-syah - Court appearance
Condiciones de la libertad - kohn-dee-SYOH-nes deh lah lee-behr-TAHD - Conditions of release
Pagar con efectivo - pah-GAHR kohn eh-fek-TEE-voh - To pay in cash
Pagar con propiedad - pah-GAHR kohn proh-pee-eh-DAHD - To pay with property
Revocación de la fianza - reh-voh-kah-SYOHN deh lah fee-AHN-sah - Revocation of bail

DIALOG

¿Cuál es el monto de la fianza para la liberación de mi cliente?
Se ha fijado una fianza de diez mil dólares.
¿Aceptan una casa como garantía para la fianza?
Sí, pero necesitamos una tasación oficial de la propiedad primero.

English translation:
What is the bail amount for my client's release?
Bail has been set at ten thousand dollars.
Do you accept a house as collateral for the bail?
Yes, but we need an official appraisal of the property first.

STORY

El juez concede la libertad provisional bajo fianza. El imputado deposita la garantía económica ante el tribunal. El auto judicial establece las medidas cautelares, incluida la prohibición de abandonar el país. El secretario judicial notifica la resolución a las partes. El acusado queda en libertad hasta la celebración del juicio, garantizando su comparecencia.

English translation: The judge grants provisional release on bail. The defendant deposits the financial guarantee with the court. The court order establishes the precautionary measures, including the prohibition to leave the country. The court clerk notifies the ruling to the parties. The accused remains free until the trial, ensuring his appearance.

PLEA BARGAIN EXPLANATIONS

Acuerdo de Declaración - ah-KWEHR-doh deh deh-klah-rah-see-OHN - Plea Agreement
Declararse Culpable - deh-klah-RAHR-seh kool-PAH-bleh - To Plead Guilty
Declararse Inocente - deh-klah-RAHR-seh ee-noh-SEN-teh - To Plead Not Guilty
Conformidad - kohn-for-mee-DAHD - Agreement (to a plea/sentence)
Negociación de la Pena - neh-goh-see-ah-see-OHN deh lah PEH-nah - Sentence Negotiation
Reducción de la Pena - reh-dook-see-OHN deh lah PEH-nah - Sentence Reduction
Cargos - KAHR-gohs - Charges
Cargos Menores - KAHR-gohs meh-NOH-res - Lesser Charges
Retirar Cargos - reh-tee-RAHR KAHR-gohs - To Drop Charges
Admisión de Hechos - ahd-mee-see-OHN deh ECH-tos - Admission of Facts
Consecuencias Legales - kohn-seh-KWEN-see-ahs leh-GAH-les - Legal Consequences
Juicio - HOO-ee-see-oh - Trial
Renuncia a Juicio - reh-NOON-see-ah ah HOO-ee-see-oh - Waiver of Trial
Declaración - deh-klah-rah-see-OHN - Plea (in court)
Sentencia - sen-TEN-see-ah - Sentence

DIALOG

¿Está dispuesto a declararse culpable a cambio de una reducción de la pena?

El fiscal ofrece retirar los cargos más graves si admite su responsabilidad.

Entiendo. ¿Cuáles serían los cargos nuevos y la sentencia recomendada?

Usted se declararía culpable de un delito menor, y nosotros recomendaremos libertad condicional.

STORY

El acusado aceptó un acuerdo de conformidad con el fiscal. A cambio de declararse culpable de un delito menor, la acusación retiró los cargos más graves. El juez revisó los términos, verificó la voluntariedad de la declaración y emitió la sentencia conforme a lo pactado, considerándolo un uso eficiente de recursos judiciales.

English translation: The defendant accepted a plea agreement with the prosecutor. In exchange for pleading guilty to a lesser offense, the prosecution dropped the more serious charges. The judge reviewed the terms, verified the voluntariness of the plea, and issued the sentence in accordance with the agreement, considering it an efficient use of judicial resources.

PROBATION TERMS

Libertad condicional - lee-behr-TAHD kohn-dee-see-oh-NAHL - Probation

Oficial de probatoria - oh-fee-SYAHL deh proh-bah-TOH-ree-ah - Probation Officer

Condiciones de la libertad condicional - kohn-dee-SYOH-nes deh lah lee-behr-TAHD kohn-dee-see-oh-NAHL - Conditions of Probation

Infracción de la probatoria - een-frahk-SYOHN deh lah proh-bah-TOH-ree-ah - Probation Violation

Audiencia de revocación - ow-DYEN-syah deh reh-boh-kah-SYOHN - Revocation Hearing

Sentencia suspendida - sen-TEN-syah soos-pen-DEE-dah - Suspended Sentence

Supervisión - soo-pehr-bee-SYOHN - Supervision

Toque de queda - TOH-keh deh KEH-dah - Curfew

Libertad bajo palabra - lee-behr-TAHD BAH-hoh pah-LAH-brah - Parole

Prueba de drogas - PRWEH-bah deh DROH-gahs - Drug Test

Servicio comunitario - sehr-BEE-syoh koh-moo-nee-TAH-ryoh - Community Service

Restitución - res-tee-too-SYOHN - Restitution

Libertad vigilada - lee-behr-TAHD bee-hee-LAH-dah - Supervised Release

Comparecencia - kohm-pah-reh-SEN-syah - Court Appearance

Orden de alejamiento - OHR-den deh ah-leh-hah-MYEN-toh - Restraining Order

DIALOG

¿Cuáles son los términos de mi libertad condicional?
Debe reportarse a su agente semanalmente y mantener empleo.
¿Qué pasa si no cumplo con estas condiciones?
La violación de estos términos resultará en una revocación de su libertad condicional.

English translation:
What are the terms of my probation?
You must report to your agent weekly and maintain employment.
What happens if I don't comply with these conditions?
Violation of these terms will result in a revocation of your probation.

STORY

El imputado aceptó los términos de la libertad condicional. El juez ordenó la supervisión del oficial de probatoria, servicio comunitario y la abstinencia de delitos. Se fijó una fianza y el acusado quedó en libertad bajo su propia responsabilidad. La sentencia definitiva queda suspendida pendiente del cumplimiento satisfactorio de estas condiciones durante el período de prueba establecido.

English translation: The defendant accepted the terms of probation. The judge ordered supervision by the probation officer, community service, and abstinence from crimes. Bail was set and the accused was released on his own recognizance. The final sentence is suspended pending the satisfactory completion of these conditions during the established probation period.

EXPUNGEMENT PROCESSES

Expediente judicial - eks-peh-DYEN-teh hoo-dee-SYAL - Court record

Expungimiento - eks-poon-hee-MYEN-toh - Expungement

Solicitud de expungimiento - soh-lee-see-TOOD deh eks-poon-hee-MYEN-toh - Expungement petition

Archivación permanente - ahr-chee-vah-SYON per-ma-NEN-teh - Permanent sealing

Rehabilitación - reh-ah-bee-lee-tah-SYON - Rehabilitation

Antecedentes penales - ahn-teh-seh-DEN-tes peh-NAH-les - Criminal record

Delito - deh-LEE-toh - Crime (less serious)

Falta - FAHL-tah - Infraction / Misdemeanor

Certificado de antecedentes penales - sehr-tee-fee-KAH-doh deh ahn-teh-seh-DEN-tes peh-NAH-les - Certificate of conduct

Audiencia - ow-DYEN-syah - Hearing

Juez - HOO-eth - Judge

Fiscal - fees-KAHL - Prosecutor

Auto judicial - OW-toh hoo-dee-SYAL - Court order

Notificación - noh-tee-fee-kah-SYON - Notification

Clausura de registro - klow-SOO-rah deh reh-HEES-troh - Sealing of the record

DIALOG

¿Cuál es el estado de mi solicitud de cancelación de antecedentes penales?
Hemos verificado que cumple con los requisitos de elegibilidad.
¿Qué significa eso para mi caso?
Su expediente será cerrado y los registros serán sellados.

English translation:
What is the status of my application for expungement of my criminal record?
We have verified that you meet the eligibility requirements.
What does that mean for my case?
Your file will be closed and the records will be sealed.

STORY

Un ciudadano solicitó la expungement de su antecedente penal. Presentó una petición ante el tribunal, argumentando su rehabilitación conforme a los estatutos aplicables. El fiscal no se opuso. Tras una audiencia, el juez concedió la orden para sellar los registros. El proceso finalizó con la notificación a las agencias pertinentes para actualizar sus archivos.

English translation: A citizen petitioned for the expungement of his criminal record. He filed a motion with the court, arguing his rehabilitation according to the applicable statutes. The prosecutor did not object. After a hearing, the judge granted the order to seal the records. The process concluded with notification to the relevant agencies to update their files.

ACCIDENT SCENE DESCRIPTIONS

Accidente - ahk-see-DEN-teh - Accident
Testigo - tes-TEE-goh - Witness
Daños materiales - DAH-nyos mah-teh-ree-AH-les - Material damages
Lesiones - leh-see-OH-nes - Injuries
Vehículo - veh-EE-koo-loh - Vehicle
Conductor - kohn-dook-TOHR - Driver
Informe policial - een-FOR-meh poh-lee-see-AHL - Police report
Culpa - KOOL-pah - Fault
Peatón - peh-ah-TOHN - Pedestrian
Semáforo - seh-MAH-foh-roh - Traffic light
Señal de tráfico - seh-NYAL deh TRAH-fee-koh - Traffic sign
Casco - KAHS-koh - Helmet
Cinturón de seguridad - seen-too-ROHN deh seh-goo-ree-DAHD - Seatbelt
Alcoholemia - ahl-koh-oh-LEH-mee-ah - Breathalyzer test
Frenar - freh-NAHR - To brake

DIALOG

¿Puede describir cómo ocurrió el accidente?
El vehículo que conducía hizo un cambio de carril brusco.
¿Testificará que no hubo intermitentes señalizando la maniobra?
Sí, testifico que no los activó.

English translation:
Can you describe how the accident happened?
The vehicle he was driving made a sudden lane change.
Will you testify that there were no turn signals indicating the maneuver?
Yes, I testify that he did not activate them.

STORY

El vehículo A impactó al vehículo B por alcance. El conductor del vehículo A declaró no haber visto las luces de freno. Los testigos corroboran la versión. Se observan daños materiales consistentes en la parte trasera del vehículo B y delantera del vehículo A. No se reportaron lesiones. Los agentes levantaron el atestado correspondiente en el lugar de los hechos.

English translation: Vehicle A impacted Vehicle B by rear-end collision. The driver of Vehicle A stated he did not see the brake lights. Witnesses corroborate the version. Material damages consistent with the rear of Vehicle B and the front of Vehicle A are observed. No injuries were reported. Officers filed the corresponding report at the scene of the incident.

MEDICAL TREATMENT AUTHORIZATION

Autorización médica - ah-toh-ree-sah-see-ON MEH-dee-kah - Medical authorization
Consentimiento informado - kon-sen-tee-MYEN-toh een-for-MAH-doh - Informed consent
Aseguradora - ah-seh-goo-rah-DOH-rah - Insurance company
Póliza de seguro - POH-lee-sah deh seh-GOO-roh - Insurance policy
Cobertura - koh-behr-TOO-rah - Coverage
Prestaciones - pres-tah-see-OH-nes - Benefits
Siniestro - see-nee-ES-troh - Claim (loss/accident)
Reclamación - reh-klah-mah-see-ON - Claim (formal demand)
Dictamen médico - deek-TAH-men MEH-dee-koh - Medical report/assessment
Incapacidad - een-kah-pah-see-DAHD - Disability
Alta médica - AHL-tah MEH-dee-kah - Medical discharge
Tratamiento - trah-tah-MYEN-toh - Treatment
Procedimiento - proh-seh-dee-MYEN-toh - Procedure
Negación de cobertura - neh-gah-see-ON deh koh-behr-TOO-rah - Denial of coverage
Apelación - ah-peh-lah-see-ON - Appeal

DIALOG

¿Autoriza usted el procedimiento médico propuesto para el menor?
Sí, doy mi consentimiento para la intervención.
¿Comprende que este documento es legalmente vinculante?
Así es, estoy conforme con los términos expuestos.

English translation:
Do you authorize the proposed medical procedure for the minor?
Yes, I give my consent for the procedure.
Do you understand that this document is legally binding?
That is correct, I am in agreement with the stated terms.

STORY

El apoderado legal, debidamente acreditado mediante poder notarial, otorga su consentimiento expreso para el procedimiento quirúrgico propuesto. Autoriza al equipo médico a realizar la intervención y actos relacionados. Reconoce haber sido informado sobre los riesgos y beneficios. Esta autorización surtirá efectos para todos los fines legales pertinentes.

English translation: The legal agent, duly accredited by notarial power, grants express consent for the proposed surgical procedure. They authorize the medical team to perform the intervention and related acts. They acknowledge having been informed of the risks and benefits. This authorization will take effect for all relevant legal purposes.

INSURANCE CLAIM TERMINOLOGY

Reclamación - reh-klah-mee-see-ON - Claim
Aseguradora - ah-seh-goo-rah-DOH-rah - Insurance Company
Asegurado - ah-seh-goo-RAH-doh - Insured
Daños - DAH-nyos - Damages
Indemnización - een-dem-nee-sah-see-ON - Compensation
Culpa - KOOL-pah - Fault
Responsabilidad civil - res-pon-sah-bee-lee-DAD see-VEEL - Civil Liability
Perito - peh-REE-toh - Adjuster / Expert Appraiser
Acta - AHK-tah - Official Report / Minutes
Siniestro - see-nee-ES-troh - Loss / Incident
Póliza de seguro - POH-lee-sah deh seh-GOO-roh - Insurance Policy
Lesiones - leh-see-OH-nes - Injuries
Derecho - deh-REH-choh - Law / Right
Prueba - PRWEH-bah - Evidence
Demanda - deh-MAN-dah - Lawsuit

DIALOG

¿Ya presentó la reclamación formal ante la aseguradora?
Sí, pero la rechazaron, alegando que no es un siniestro cubierto.
Entonces, procederemos a interponer la demanda por mala fe contractual.
Necesitaré su poder notarial para representarle ante el tribunal.

English translation:
Did you already file the formal claim with the insurer?
Yes, but they rejected it, arguing it is not a covered loss.
Then, we will proceed to file the lawsuit for contractual bad faith.
I will need your notarized power of attorney to represent you before the court.

STORY

El asegurado presentó una reclamación por daños a la propiedad tras el siniestro. La compañía de seguros designó un perito para evaluar los daños y determinar la indemnización correspondiente. Tras verificar la póliza y la documentación, se procedió al pago por la pérdida total, cerrando el siniestro conforme a los términos establecidos en las condiciones generales.

English translation: The policyholder filed a property damage claim following the incident. The insurance company appointed an adjuster to assess the damages and determine the corresponding compensation. After verifying the policy and documentation, payment was made for the total loss, closing the claim according to the terms set in the policy conditions.

SETTLEMENT NEGOTIATIONS

Acuerdo - ah-KWEHR-doh - Agreement
Cláusula - KLAU-soo-lah - Clause
Confidencialidad - kohn-fee-den-see-ah-lee-DAHD - Confidentiality
Daños y perjuicios - DAH-nyos ee pehr-HWEE-see-os - Damages
Demandante - deh-mahn-DAN-teh - Plaintiff
Demandado - deh-mahn-DAH-doh - Defendant
Indemnización - een-dem-nee-sah-see-ON - Indemnity
Liberación de responsabilidad - lee-beh-rah-see-ON deh reh-spon-sah-bee-lee-DAHD - Release of liability
Monto - MOHN-toh - Amount
Negociación - neh-goh-see-ah-see-ON - Negotiation
Pago único - PAH-goh OO-nee-koh - Lump sum payment
Parte interesada - PAR-teh een-teh-reh-SA-dah - Interested party
Resolución - reh-soh-loo-see-ON - Settlement
Transacción - trahn-sahk-see-ON - Transaction/Settlement
Válido - VAH-lee-doh - Valid

DIALOG

Propongo una compensación de cincuenta mil euros para resolver el asunto.

Necesito una garantía por escrito de que esto cierra todas las reclamaciones futuras.

Por supuesto, el acuerdo de conciliación incluirá una cláusula de renuncia a futuras acciones.

Acepto la propuesta. Procederemos con la redacción del convenio.

English translation:

I propose a compensation of fifty thousand euros to resolve the matter.

I need a written guarantee that this settles all future claims.

Of course, the settlement agreement will include a clause waiving future legal action.

I accept the proposal. We will proceed with drafting the agreement.

STORY

El demandante presentó una oferta de conciliación para resolver la controversia contractual. La parte demandada la aceptó, reconociendo la obligación de indemnizar por daños y perjuicios. Se redactó un acta de transacción detallando los términos del acuerdo, incluyendo el monto y el plazo de pago. Ambas partes firmaron el documento, poniendo fin al litigio pendiente.

English translation: The plaintiff presented a settlement offer to resolve the contractual dispute. The defendant accepted it, acknowledging the obligation to compensate for damages. A settlement agreement was drafted detailing the terms of the agreement, including the amount and payment deadline. Both parties signed the document, ending the pending litigation.

PAIN AND SUFFERING EXPLANATIONS

Dolor - doh-LOR - Pain
Sufrimiento - soo-free-MYEN-toh - Suffering
Daño - DAH-nyo - Damage/Harm
Lesión - leh-SYON - Injury
Padecimiento - pah-deh-see-MYEN-toh - Affliction
Agravio - ah-GRAH-vyoh - Grievance/Harm
Perjuicio - pehr-HWEE-syoh - Detriment/Loss
Trastorno - trahs-TOR-noh - Disorder
Discapacidad - dees-kah-pah-see-DAHD - Disability
Incapacidad - een-kah-pah-see-DAHD - Incapacity
Secuela - seh-KWEH-lah - Sequela/Aftermath
Trauma - TRAU-mah - Trauma
Angustia - ahn-GOOS-tyah - Anguish
Pérdida - PEHR-dee-dah - Loss
Afectación - ah-fek-tah-SYON - Impairment

DIALOG

El demandante alega daños morales por el dolor y sufrimiento padecido.
¿Qué pruebas documentales respaldan dicha afirmación?
Presentamos informes médicos y declaraciones juradas que detallan el impacto psicológico.
Procederemos a evaluar la legitimidad de estas pruebas para determinar la indemnización.

English translation:
The plaintiff alleges moral damages for the pain and suffering endured.
What documentary evidence supports that claim?
We are submitting medical reports and sworn statements detailing the psychological impact.
We will proceed to evaluate the legitimacy of this evidence to determine the compensation.

STORY

El demandante sufrió lesiones graves en el accidente. La parte demandada alega fuerza mayor. El perito médico documentó el daño físico y el tratamiento. El juez evaluará la prueba pericial y los testimonios para determinar la indemnización por daños y perjuicios, considerando la negligencia y el nexo causal.

English translation: The plaintiff suffered serious injuries in the accident. The defendant alleges force majeure. The medical expert documented the physical harm and treatment. The judge will evaluate the expert evidence and testimonies to determine compensation for damages, considering negligence and causation.

PROPERTY PURCHASE CONTRACTS

Compraventa - kohm-prah-VEN-tah - Purchase and Sale
Contrato de arras - kohn-TRAH-toh deh AH-rahs - Earnest Money Contract
Depósito de garantía - deh-POH-see-toh deh gah-rahn-TEE-ah - Security Deposit
Escritura pública - es-kree-TOO-rah POO-blee-kah - Public Deed
Fiador - fee-ah-DOR - Guarantor
Hipoteca - ee-poh-TEH-kah - Mortgage
Plazo de desistimiento - PLAH-soh deh deh-sees-tee-mee-EN-toh - Withdrawal Period
Notario - noh-TAH-ree-oh - Notary Public
Oferta - oh-FEHR-tah - Offer
Propiedad - proh-pee-eh-DAHD - Property
Registro de la Propiedad - reh-HEES-troh deh lah proh-pee-eh-DAHD - Land Registry
Reserva - reh-SEHR-vah - Reservation
Tasa Anual Equivalente (TAE) - TAH-sah ah-NWAHL eh-kee-vah-LEN-teh - Annual Equivalent Rate (AER)
Título de propiedad - TEE-too-loh deh proh-pee-eh-DAHD - Title Deed
Valor catastral - vah-LOR kah-tahs-TRAHL - Cadastral Value

DIALOG

¿Está conforme con las cláusulas de arras pactadas en el contrato?
Sí, acepto la penalización por desistimiento.
Perfecto. Firmemos el documento de compraventa ante notario.
De acuerdo. Procedamos con la firma.

English translation:
Are you in agreement with the penalty clause terms stipulated in the contract?
Yes, I accept the withdrawal penalty.
Perfect. Let us sign the deed of sale before a notary.
Agreed. Let us proceed with the signing.

STORY

El comprador y el vendedor suscribieron el contrato de compraventa ante notario. El inmueble fue descrito en la escritura pública, incluyendo su inscripción registral. El precio pactado se pagó mediante transferencia bancaria. Se adjuntó el certificado de eficiencia energética. Ambas partes manifestaron su conformidad y la ausencia de cargas o gravámenes no declarados.

English translation: The buyer and the seller executed the sale contract before a notary. The property was described in the public deed, including its land registry details. The agreed price was paid by bank transfer. The energy performance certificate was attached. Both parties declared their agreement and the absence of any undeclared encumbrances or liens.

LEASE AGREEMENT EXPLANATIONS

Arrendador - ah-ren-dah-DOR - Lessor/Landlord
Arrendatario - ah-ren-dah-TAH-ryoh - Lessee/Tenant
Contrato de Arrendamiento - kon-TRAH-toh deh ah-ren-dah-MYEN-toh - Lease Agreement
Plazo - PLAH-soh - Term/Duration
Renta - REN-tah - Rent
Depósito de Garantía - deh-POH-see-toh deh gah-rahn-TEE-ah - Security Deposit
Cláusula - KLAU-soo-lah - Clause
Obligaciones - oh-blee-gah-see-OH-nes - Obligations
Derechos - deh-REH-chos - Rights
Propiedad - proh-pyeh-DAHD - Property
Mantenimiento - mahn-teh-nee-MYEN-toh - Maintenance
Incumplimiento - een-kum-plee-MYEN-toh - Breach/Non-compliance
Rescisión - reh-see-SYON - Termination
Fianza - FYAN-sah - Security Deposit (common synonym)
Uso - OO-soh - Use/Purpose

DIALOG

¿Podría explicarme la cláusula de terminación anticipada?
Esta cláusula detalla las condiciones y multas por finalizar el contrato antes de la fecha acordada.
Entiendo. ¿Y el depósito de garantía se devuelve en ese caso?
Sí, pero se deducirán los gastos por daños o pagos pendientes, según lo estipulado.

English translation:
Could you explain the early termination clause to me?
This clause details the conditions and penalties for ending the contract before the agreed-upon date.
I understand. And is the security deposit returned in that case?
Yes, but costs for damages or outstanding payments will be deducted, as stipulated.

STORY

El arrendador otorga el uso del inmueble al arrendatario, quien se obliga al pago de la renta. El contrato de arrendamiento establece el plazo, la fianza y las cargas. El incumplimiento de las obligaciones contractuales puede dar lugar a la resolución del contrato y a la reclamación de daños y perjuicios conforme a la ley.

English translation: The lessor grants use of the property to the lessee, who is obligated to pay rent. The lease agreement establishes the term, the security deposit, and the charges. Breach of contractual obligations may lead to termination of the contract and a claim for damages pursuant to the law.

ZONING LAW CONSULTATIONS

Zonificación - soh-nee-fee-kah-see-OHN - Zoning
Uso de suelo - OO-soh deh SWEH-loh - Land use
Permiso de construcción - pehr-MEE-soh deh kohn-strook-see-OHN - Building permit
Licencia urbanística - lee-SEN-see-ah oor-bah-NEES-tee-kah - Urban development license
Plan parcial - plahn pahr-see-AHL - Partial plan
Normativa urbanística - nor-mah-TEE-bah oor-bah-NEES-tee-kah - Urban planning regulations
Densidad - den-see-DAHD - Density
Alineación - ah-lee-neh-ah-see-OHN - Setback / Building line
Altura máxima - ahl-TOO-rah MAHK-see-mah - Maximum height
Cesión de suelo - seh-see-OHN deh SWEH-loh - Land dedication
Clasificación del suelo - klah-see-fee-kah-see-OHN dehl SWEH-loh - Land classification
Calificación urbanística - kah-lee-fee-kah-see-OHN oor-bah-NEES-tee-kah - Urban qualification
Edificabilidad - eh-dee-fee-kah-bee-lee-DAHD - Buildability
Ordenanza municipal - or-deh-NAN-sah moo-nee-see-PAHL - Municipal ordinance
Estudio de impacto ambiental - ehs-TOO-dee-oh deh eem-PAHK-toh ahm-bee-EN-tahl - Environmental impact study

DIALOG

¿Cuál es el uso permitido para un terreno clasificado como residencial unifamiliar?
Se permite solo una vivienda independiente por parcela, según el plan de ordenamiento urbano.
¿Se podría solicitar una variación para subdividir la propiedad?
Sí, pero requiere presentar una solicitud de excepción y obtener la aprobación municipal.

English translation:
What is the permitted use for a lot zoned as single-family residential?
Only one detached dwelling per parcel is allowed, according to the urban planning code.
Could one apply for a variance to subdivide the property?
Yes, but it requires filing an exception request and obtaining municipal approval.

STORY

Un promotor urbano consultó sobre la normativa de zonificación municipal. Se analizó el plan general para verificar los usos permitidos en el terreno. Se confirmó que el proyecto propuesto cumplía con la ordenanza vigente. Se redactó un informe jurídico detallado para presentar ante la comisión de urbanismo, asegurando la viabilidad del desarrollo.

English translation: An urban developer consulted on the municipal zoning regulations. The general plan was analyzed to verify the permitted uses of the land. It was confirmed that the proposed project complied with the current ordinance. A detailed legal report was drafted to present before the urban planning commission, ensuring the development's viability.

EMINENT DOMAIN DISCUSSIONS

Dominio eminente - doh-MEE-nee-oh eh-mee-NEN-teh - Eminent domain
Expropiación - eks-proh-pee-ah-SYON - Expropriation
Propiedad - proh-pee-eh-DAHD - Property
Bienes raíces - BYEH-nes rah-EE-ses - Real estate
Indemnización - een-dem-nee-sah-SYON - Compensation
Valor de mercado - vah-LOR deh mehr-KAH-doh - Market value
Utilidad pública - oo-tee-lee-DAHD POO-blee-kah - Public use
Notificación - noh-tee-fee-kah-SYON - Notice
Audiencia - ow-DYEN-syah - Hearing
Proceso judicial - proh-SEH-so hoo-dee-SYAHL - Judicial process
Toma de posesión - TOH-mah deh poh-seh-SYON - Taking possession
Justiprecio - hoos-tee-PREH-syoh - Appraisal
Servidumbre - sehr-vee-DOOM-breh - Easement
Daños y perjuicios - DAH-nyos ee pehr-HWEE-syohs - Damages
Orden de desalojo - OR-den deh deh-sah-LOH-hoh - Eviction order

DIALOG

¿Está el gobierno realmente autorizado a tomar mi propiedad contra mi voluntad?
Sí, mediante el poder de expropiación por causa de utilidad pública, previa indemnización.
Pero el precio que ofrecen no refleja el valor real del terreno.
Puede impugnar la oferta y solicitar una valoración pericial independiente.

English translation:
Is the government really authorized to take my property against my will?
Yes, through the power of eminent domain for public use, with prior compensation.
But the price they offer doesn't reflect the real value of the land.
You can challenge the offer and request an independent expert appraisal.

STORY

El municipio inició un procedimiento de expropiación forzosa por utilidad pública. Notificó a los propietarios la declaración de necesidad de ocupación. Se depositó la indemnización en la Caja de Depósitos. Los titulares de los derechos afectados interpusieron un recurso contencioso-administrativo, alegando una valoración injusta del justiprecio. El juez admitió la demanda a trámite.

English translation: The municipality initiated a forced expropriation procedure for public utility. It notified the owners of the declaration of necessity of occupation. The compensation was deposited in the Deposits and Consignments Fund. The holders of the affected rights filed an administrative appeal, alleging an unfair valuation of the fair price. The judge admitted the lawsuit for processing.

TITLE SEARCH EXPLANATIONS

Jurisdicción - hoo-rees-DEEK-see-on - Jurisdiction
Demanda - deh-MAN-dah - Lawsuit
Demandado - deh-man-DAH-doh - Defendant
Demandante - deh-man-DAN-teh - Plaintiff
Testamento - tes-tah-MEN-toh - Will
Poder - poh-DEHR - Power of Attorney
Hipoteca - ee-poh-TEH-kah - Mortgage
Embargo - em-BAR-goh - Lien
Escritura - es-kree-TOO-rah - Deed
Contrato - kon-TRAH-toh - Contract
Sentencia - sen-TEN-see-ah - Judgment
Apelación - ah-peh-lah-see-ON - Appeal
Título - TEE-too-loh - Title
Gravamen - grah-VAH-men - Encumbrance
Propiedad - proh-pee-eh-DAHD - Property

DIALOG

¿Puede explicarme qué es una búsqueda de título?
Consiste en revisar los registros públicos para verificar la propiedad de un bien inmueble.
¿Qué documentos suelen revisar en este proceso?
Principalmente escrituras notariales y las anotaciones en el Registro de la Propiedad.

English translation:
Can you explain to me what a title search is?
It involves reviewing public records to verify the ownership of a real estate property.
What documents do you usually review in this process?
Mainly notarial deeds and the annotations in the Property Registry.

STORY

El abogado consultó la jurisprudencia en la base de datos legal. Utilizó términos de búsqueda específicos para localizar sentencias relevantes. Encontró un precedente sobre la responsabilidad contractual. El fallo aclaró los requisitos de la obligación de medios. Esto fue crucial para la estrategia de su demanda.

English translation: The lawyer consulted case law in the legal database. He used specific search terms to locate relevant rulings. He found a precedent on contractual liability. The ruling clarified the requirements for the obligation of means. This was crucial for his lawsuit strategy.

WRONGFUL TERMINATION TERMS

Despido injustificado - dess-PEE-doh een-hoos-tee-fee-KAH-doh - Wrongful termination
Despido improcedente - dess-PEE-doh eem-proh-sen-DEN-teh - Unfair dismissal
Despido nulo - dess-PEE-doh NOO-loh - Null dismissal
Despido disciplinario - dess-PEE-doh dee-see-plee-nah-ree-oh - Disciplinary dismissal
Indemnización por despido - een-dem-nee-sah-see-ON por dess-PEE-doh - Dismissal compensation
Finiquito - fee-nee-KEE-toh - Final settlement
Preaviso - preh-ah-VEE-soh - Notice
Causa justificada - KOW-sah hoos-tee-fee-KAH-dah - Just cause
Mobbing - MOH-beeng - Workplace harassment
Acoso laboral - ah-KOH-soh lah-boh-RAHL - Workplace bullying
Reclamación - reh-klah-mah-see-ON - Claim
Demanda laboral - deh-MAN-dah lah-boh-RAHL - Labor lawsuit
Conciliación - kon-see-lee-ah-see-ON - Conciliation
Acta de conciliación - AHK-tah deh kon-see-lee-ah-see-ON - Conciliation minutes
Reinstalación - reh-een-stah-lah-see-ON - Reinstatement

DIALOG

¿Se considera mi despido como improcedente según el artículo 55 del Estatuto de los Trabajadores?
Sí, porque la empresa no ha acreditado las causas alegadas para el finiquito.
Entonces, ¿tengo derecho a una indemnización por despido improcedente?
Correcto, le corresponde una indemnización de treinta y tres días por año trabajado.

English translation:
Is my termination considered wrongful according to article 55 of the Workers' Statute?
Yes, because the company has not proven the alleged reasons for the severance.
So, do I have the right to compensation for wrongful termination?
Correct, you are entitled to compensation of thirty-three days per year worked.

STORY

El trabajador interpuso una demanda por despido improcedente. Alegó que la empresa no acreditó la causa disciplinaria ni siguió el procedimiento sancionador establecido. Solicitó la readmisión y el pago de salarios de tramitación. El juez, tras analizar el caso, declaró la nulidad del despido y condenó al empleador a las indemnizaciones correspondientes.

English translation: The worker filed a lawsuit for wrongful termination. He alleged the company did not prove the disciplinary cause or follow the established sanctioning procedure. He requested reinstatement and payment of back wages. The judge, after analyzing the case, declared the dismissal null and ordered the employer to pay the corresponding compensation.

WORKPLACE DISCRIMINATION

Acoso laboral - ah-KOH-soh lah-boh-RAHL - Workplace harassment
Discriminación - dees-kree-mee-nah-see-ON - Discrimination
Hostigamiento - ohs-tee-gah-MYEN-toh - Harassment
Acoso sexual - ah-KOH-soh sek-SWAHL - Sexual harassment
Represalia - reh-preh-SAHL-ee-ah - Retaliation
Despido injustificado - des-PEE-doh een-hoos-tee-fee-KAH-doh - Wrongful termination
Igualdad de oportunidades - ee-gwahl-DAD deh oh-poor-too-nee-DAH-des - Equal opportunity
Entorno hostil - en-TOR-noh ohs-TEEL - Hostile work environment
Discriminación por edad - dees-kree-mee-nah-see-ON por eh-DAD - Age discrimination
Discriminación por género - dees-kree-mee-nah-see-ON por HEN-eh-roh - Gender discrimination
Acoso por razón de sexo - ah-KOH-soh por rah-SON deh SEK-soh - Harassment on the grounds of sex
Indemnización - een-dem-nee-sah-see-ON - Compensation
Reintegro laboral - reh-een-TEH-groh lah-boh-RAHL - Reinstatement
Conciliación laboral - kon-see-lee-ah-see-ON lah-boh-RAHL - Labor conciliation
Denuncia - deh-NOON-see-ah - Complaint

DIALOG

No me dieron el ascenso a pesar de tener más experiencia y los mejores resultados.
La decisión se basó en la necesidad de un perfil diferente para el puesto.
¿Un perfil diferente? Los únicos candidatos promovidos son más jóvenes y sin mi antigüedad.
Presentaré una queja formal por discriminación por edad ante el comité.

English translation:
I didn't get the promotion despite having more experience and the best results.
The decision was based on the need for a different profile for the position.
A different profile? The only candidates promoted are younger and don't have my seniority.
I will file a formal complaint for age discrimination with the committee.

STORY

La abogada senior presentó una demanda por discriminación laboral. Alegó trato desigual en la asignación de casos complejos y en la promoción a socia. La firma legal negó las acusaciones, citando méritos. El juez admitió la prueba testifcial y documental. El caso se resolvió mediante un acuerdo conciliatorio confidencial antes del veredicto.

English translation: The senior lawyer filed a workplace discrimination lawsuit. She alleged unequal treatment in the assignment of complex cases and in promotion to partner. The law firm denied the allegations, citing merits. The judge admitted testimonial and documentary evidence. The case was resolved through a confidential settlement agreement before the verdict.

SEVERANCE PACKAGE NEGOTIATIONS

Paquete de indemnización - pah-KEH-teh deh een-deh-mee-nah-see-OHN - Severance package

Negociación - neh-goh-see-ah-see-OHN - Negotiation

Finiquito - fee-nee-KEE-toh - Full and final settlement

Indemnización por despido - een-deh-mee-nah-see-OHN por dehs-PEE-doh - Dismissal compensation

Preaviso - preh-ah-BEE-soh - Notice period

Liquidación - lee-kee-dah-see-OHN - Severance pay calculation

Cláusula de confidencialidad - KLAU-soo-lah deh kon-fee-den-see-ah-lee-DAHD - Confidentiality clause

Cláusula de no competencia - KLAU-soo-lah deh no kom-peh-TEN-see-ah - Non-compete clause

Renuncia voluntaria - reh-NOON-see-ah vo-loon-TAH-ree-ah - Voluntary resignation

Despido improcedente - dehs-PEE-doh eem-proh-seh-DEN-teh - Unfair dismissal

Convenio - kon-VEH-nyoh - Settlement agreement

Baja voluntaria - BAH-hah vo-loon-TAH-ree-ah - Voluntary termination

Acuerdo mutuo - ah-KWEHR-doh MOO-too-oh - Mutual agreement

Extinción de contrato - eks-teen-see-OHN deh kon-TRAH-toh - Termination of contract

Referencia laboral - reh-feh-REN-see-ah lah-boh-RAHL - Employment reference

DIALOG

Le propongo una indemnización equivalente a doce meses de salario, más la bonificación anual.
Considero que dieciocho meses sería más apropiado, dados mis años de servicio y el despido improcedente.
Incluiré la cobertura médica extendida por seis meses, pero la indemnización se mantiene en doce.
Acepto los doce meses, con la condición de que se incluya una carta de recomendación firmada.

English translation:
I am offering a severance package equivalent to twelve months of salary, plus the annual bonus.
I believe eighteen months would be more appropriate, given my years of service and the wrongful termination.
I will include extended medical coverage for six months, but the severance remains at twelve.
I accept the twelve months, on the condition that a signed letter of recommendation is included.

STORY

El abogado presentó su renuncia. Inició la negociación de su indemnización por despido. Solicitó el pago íntegro de sus partes variables y la prórroga de su seguro médico. La empresa ofreció un monto global a cambio de una renuncia a reclamos. Finalmente, firmaron un acuerdo de confidencialidad y una cláusula de no competencia por doce meses.

English translation: The lawyer submitted his resignation. He began negotiating his severance package. He requested full payment of his variable bonuses and an extension of his health insurance. The company offered a lump sum in exchange for a release of claims. Finally, they signed a confidentiality agreement and a non-compete clause for twelve months.

NON-COMPETE AGREEMENTS

Acuerdo de no competencia - ah-KWER-doh deh noh kohm-peh-TEN-see-ah - Non-compete agreement
Confidencialidad - kohn-fee-den-see-ah-lee-DAHD - Confidentiality
Cláusula de no competencia - KLAU-soo-lah deh noh kohm-peh-TEN-see-ah - Non-compete clause
Secreto comercial - seh-KREH-toh koh-mehr-see-AHL - Trade secret
Duración - doo-rah-see-OHN - Duration
Ámbito geográfico - AHM-bee-toh heh-oh-GRAH-fee-koh - Geographic scope
Actividades restringidas - ahk-tee-bee-DAH-dehs res-treen-HEE-dahs - Restricted activities
Indemnización por daños - een-dehm-nee-sah-see-OHN pohr DAH-nyohs - Damages
Injunción - een-hoonk-see-OHN - Injunction
Incumplimiento - een-koom-plee-mee-EN-toh - Breach
Rescisión - reh-see-see-OHN - Termination
Legítimo interés comercial - leh-HEE-tee-moh een-teh-REHS koh-mehr-see-AHL - Legitimate business interest
Consideración - kohn-see-deh-rah-see-OHN - Consideration
Pacto de no concurrencia - PAHK-toh deh noh kohn-koo-RREN-see-ah - Covenant not to compete
Relación laboral - reh-lah-see-OHN lah-boh-RAHL - Employment relationship

DIALOG

¿El acuerdo de no competencia que firmé es válido indefinidamente?
No, según la ley, tiene una duración máxima de dos años.
¿Qué pasa si incumplo el acuerdo?
Podrías enfrentar una demanda por daños y perjuicios.

English translation:
Is the non-compete agreement I signed valid indefinitely?
No, according to the law, it has a maximum duration of two years.
What happens if I breach the agreement?
You could face a lawsuit for damages.

STORY

Un abogado firmó un pacto de no competencia al dejar su firma. El acuerdo estipulaba una cláusula de no competir con clientes de la firma por un año. El abogado inició una nueva práctica, respetando las restricciones convenidas. Cumplió con el plazo de vigencia y sus obligaciones contractuales, evitando cualquier conflicto de intereses con su anterior empleador.

English translation: A lawyer signed a non-compete agreement upon leaving his firm. The agreement stipulated a clause not to compete with the firm's clients for one year. The lawyer started a new practice, respecting the agreed restrictions. He complied with the term of validity and his contractual obligations, avoiding any conflict of interest with his former employer.

WORKERS' COMPENSATION CLAIMS

Accidente de trabajo - ahk-see-DEN-teh deh trah-BAH-ho - Work accident
Enfermedad profesional - en-fehr-meh-DAHD pro-feh-see-oh-nal - Occupational disease
Indemnización - een-dem-nee-sah-see-ON - Compensation
Incapacidad temporal - een-kah-pah-see-DAD tem-poh-RAL - Temporary disability
Incapacidad permanente - een-kah-pah-see-DAD pehr-mah-NEN-teh - Permanent disability
Reclamación - reh-klah-mah-see-ON - Claim
Lesión - leh-see-ON - Injury
Jubilación por incapacidad - hoo-bee-lah-see-ON por een-kah-pah-see-DAD - Disability retirement
Alta médica - AHL-tah MEH-dee-kah - Medical discharge (return to work)
Baja médica - BAH-hah MEH-dee-kah - Medical leave (sick note)
Secuela - seh-KWEH-lah - Sequela (lasting effect of injury)
Rehabilitación - reh-ah-bee-lee-tah-see-ON - Rehabilitation
Daños y perjuicios - DAH-nyos ee pehr-HWEE-see-os - Damages
Parte de accidente - PAR-teh deh ahk-see-DEN-teh - Accident report
Dictamen médico - deek-TAH-men MEH-dee-ko - Medical opinion/report

DIALOG

¿Presentó ya la reclamación de compensación laboral ante la junta?
Sí, presenté el formulario de reclamación la semana pasada.
¿Incluyó todos los informes médicos como evidencia?
Sí, adjunté todos los documentos que detallan la lesión y el tratamiento.

English translation:
Have you already filed the workers' compensation claim with the board?
Yes, I filed the claim form last week.
Did you include all the medical reports as evidence?
Yes, I attached all the documents detailing the injury and the treatment.

STORY

El trabajador sufrió una lesión lumbar durante el manejo manual de carga. Se presentó el parte de accidente inmediatamente. La evaluación médica confirmó una distensión muscular. El tratamiento incluye fisioterapia y reposo laboral temporal. La empleadora inició el trámite de reclamación ante la aseguradora para cubrir los gastos médicos y la indemnización por incapacidad temporal conforme a la ley.

English translation: The worker suffered a lumbar injury during the manual handling of cargo. The accident report was filed immediately. The medical evaluation confirmed a muscle strain. Treatment includes physical therapy and temporary work rest. The employer initiated the claim process with the insurer to cover medical expenses and temporary disability compensation according to the law.

WILL PREPARATION TERMS

Testamento - teh-stah-MEN-toh - Will
Testador - teh-stah-DOR - Testator
Heredero - eh-reh-DEH-ro - Heir
Legado - leh-GAH-doh - Bequest
Albacea - ahl-bah-SEH-ah - Executor
Beneficiario - beh-neh-fee-see-AH-ryo - Beneficiary
Última Voluntad - OOL-tee-mah voh-loon-TAHD - Last Will
Herencia - eh-REN-see-ah - Inheritance
Testigo - teh-STEE-goh - Witness
Notario - noh-TAH-ryo - Notary Public
Capacidad Testamentaria - kah-pah-see-DAHD teh-stah-men-TAH-ryah - Testamentary Capacity
Legítima - leh-HEE-tee-mah - Forced Heirship Portion
Cláusula - KLAU-soo-lah - Clause
Revocación - reh-voh-kah-see-ON - Revocation
Codicilo - koh-dee-SEE-loh - Codicil

DIALOG

¿Está conforme con nombrar a su cónyuge como heredero universal?
Sí, así lo deseo. Que herede todos mis bienes.
Muy bien. ¿Y quién designa como albacea testamentario?
Designo a mi hermano para que se encargue de cumplir mis últimas voluntades.

English translation:
Are you in agreement with naming your spouse as your universal heir?
Yes, that is my wish. That they inherit all my assets.
Very well. And who do you appoint as the executor of the will?
I appoint my brother to be in charge of carrying out my last wishes.

STORY

El testador otorga testamento ante notario. Designa herederos universales y un legatario. Nombra un albacea para cumplir su última voluntad. Incluye cláusulas específicas sobre su patrimonio. El notario autoriza el instrumento, asegurando que cumple con los requisitos legales. Los testigos firman el documento. Así, la sucesión testamentaria queda formalmente establecida.

English translation: The testator executes a will before a notary. He designates universal heirs and a legatee. He names an executor to fulfill his last will. It includes specific clauses about his estate. The notary authorizes the instrument, ensuring it meets legal requirements. The witnesses sign the document. Thus, the testate succession is formally established.

TRUST FUND EXPLANATIONS

Fideicomiso - fee-day-koh-MEE-soh - Trust Fund
Fideicomitente - fee-day-koh-mee-TEN-teh - Settlor/Trustor
Fiduciario - fee-doo-see-AH-ree-oh - Trustee
Beneficiario - beh-neh-fee-see-AH-ree-oh - Beneficiary
Patrimonio - pah-tree-MOH-nee-oh - Estate/Assets
Bienes - bee-EH-nes - Assets/Goods
Administración - ahd-mee-nee-strah-see-ON - Administration
Rendición de Cuentas - ren-dee-see-ON deh Kwen-tahs - Accounting
Cláusula - KLAU-soo-lah - Clause
Testamento - tes-tah-MEN-toh - Will
Herencia - eh-REN-see-ah - Inheritance
Mandato - mahn-DAH-toh - Mandate/Instruction
Disposición - dees-poh-see-see-ON - Disposition/Provision
Finalidad - fee-nah-lee-DAHD - Purpose
Distribución - dees-tree-boo-see-ON - Distribution

DIALOG

¿Podría explicarme en qué consiste exactamente un fideicomiso?
Un fideicomiso es un acuerdo legal donde un fiduciario administra bienes para un beneficiario.
Entiendo. ¿Y cuáles son las obligaciones principales del fiduciario?
El fiduciario debe gestionar los bienes con prudencia y siempre en el mejor interés del beneficiario.

English translation:
Could you explain to me what a trust fund consists of, exactly?
A trust fund is a legal agreement where a trustee manages assets for a beneficiary.
I understand. And what are the main obligations of the trustee?
The trustee must manage the assets prudently and always in the best interest of the beneficiary.

STORY

El fideicomiso se constituyó mediante escritura pública. El fiduciante transfirió los bienes al fiduciario, quien los administrará para el beneficiario. El fideicomisario supervisa el cumplimiento del fin establecido. Los activos en custodia están protegidos contra reclamaciones de acreedores, de conformidad con la ley aplicable.

English translation: The trust was established via a public deed. The settlor transferred the assets to the trustee, who will administer them for the beneficiary. The trust protector oversees compliance with the established purpose. The assets in custody are protected from creditor claims, in accordance with applicable law.

POWER OF ATTORNEY TYPES

Poder general - poh-DEHR heh-neh-RAHL - General power of attorney

Poder especial - poh-DEHR es-peh-see-AHL - Special power of attorney

Poder notarial - poh-DEHR noh-tah-ree-AHL - Notarized power of attorney

Poder para pleitos - poh-DEHR PAH-rah PLAY-tohs - Power of attorney for lawsuits

Poder para actos de administración - poh-DEHR PAH-rah AHK-tohs deh ahd-mee-nees-trah-see-ON - Power of attorney for administrative acts

Poder para contratar - poh-DEHR PAH-rah kon-trah-TAHR - Power of attorney to contract

Apoderado - ah-poh-deh-RAH-doh - Attorney-in-fact / Agent

Poderdante - poh-dehr-DAHN-teh - Principal / Grantor

Poder en vida - poh-DEHR en VEE-dah - Power of attorney during life

Poder durable - poh-DEHR doo-RAH-bleh - Durable power of attorney

Poder para cuidados de salud - poh-DEHR PAH-rah kwee-DAH-dohs deh sah-LOOD - Power of attorney for healthcare

Poder notario - poh-DEHR noh-TAH-ree-oh - Notary public

Revocación - reh-voh-kah-see-ON - Revocation

Poder suficiente - poh-DEHR soo-fee-see-EN-teh - Sufficient power of attorney

Poder amplio - poh-DEHR AHM-plee-oh - Broad power of

attorney

DIALOG

¿Está listo para otorgar el poder notarial general?
Sí, pero necesito que incluya una cláusula específica para la venta de propiedades.
De acuerdo, la añadiremos al documento como una disposición especial.
Perfecto. Procedamos entonces con la firma ante el notario.

English translation:
Are you ready to grant the general power of attorney?
Yes, but I need you to include a specific clause for the sale of properties.
Agreed, we will add it to the document as a special provision.
Perfect. Let us then proceed with the signing before the notary.

STORY

El apoderado, designado mediante poder notarial, ejerce la representación legal del poderdante. Gestiona asuntos financieros y patrimoniales según los términos del mandato. El poder, debidamente otorgado e inscrito, faculta al apoderado para realizar actos jurídicos en nombre del principal, asegurando el cumplimiento de su voluntad dentro del marco legal establecido.

English translation: The attorney-in-fact, appointed via notarized power of attorney, exercises the principal's legal representation. They manage financial and patrimonial matters according to the mandate's terms. The power, duly granted and registered, authorizes the agent to perform legal acts on behalf of the principal, ensuring the fulfillment of their will within the established legal framework.

ESTATE TAX DISCUSSIONS

Impuesto sobre Sucesiones - eem-PWES-toh soh-breh soo-seh-SYO-nes - Estate Tax
Testamento - tes-tah-MEN-toh - Will
Herencia - eh-REN-see-ah - Inheritance
Legítima - leh-HEE-tee-mah - Forced Heirship Portion
Albacea - ahl-bah-SEH-ah - Executor
Heredero - eh-reh-DEH-ro - Heir
Legatario - leh-gah-TAH-ree-oh - Legatee
Beneficiario - beh-neh-fee-see-AH-ree-oh - Beneficiary
Base Imponible - BAH-seh eem-poh-NEE-bleh - Taxable Base
Declaración de Herederos - deh-klah-rah-SYON deh eh-reh-DEH-ros - Declaration of Heirs
Plazo de Declaración - PLAH-soh deh deh-klah-rah-SYON - Filing Deadline
Bonificación - boh-nee-fee-kah-SYON - Tax Allowance
Deducción - deh-dook-SYON - Deduction
Valor Catastral - vah-LOR kah-tahs-TRAHL - Cadastral Value
Usufructo - oo-soo-FROOK-toh - Usufruct

DIALOG

¿Ya presentó la declaración del impuesto de sucesiones?
No, aún estamos recopilando los documentos de los bienes heredados.
Recuerde que el plazo para presentarla es de seis meses desde el fallecimiento.
Entiendo, nos aseguraremos de cumplir con el plazo para evitar sanciones.

English translation:
Have you already filed the estate tax return?
No, we are still gathering the documents for the inherited assets.
Remember that the deadline to file it is six months from the date of death.
I understand, we will ensure we meet the deadline to avoid penalties.

STORY

Un testador otorgó testamento ante notario, designando herederos universales. Tras su fallecimiento, se inició la sucesión. Los albaceas liquidaron el impuesto sobre sucesiones ante la administración tributaria. La base imponible incluyó el patrimonio total, aplicándose la deducción por parentesco. La herencia se adjudicó a los herederos una vez obtenida la liquidación.

English translation: A testator executed a will before a notary, designating universal heirs. Upon death, the succession process began. The executors settled the estate tax with the tax authority. The tax base included the total estate, applying the kinship deduction. The inheritance was distributed to the heirs once the tax clearance was obtained.

INHERITANCE DISPUTES

Herencia - eh-REN-see-ah - Inheritance
Testamento - tes-tah-MEN-toh - Will
Testamento ológrafo - tes-tah-MEN-toh oh-LOH-grah-foh - Holographic will
Legítima - leh-HEE-tee-mah - Compulsory share
Heredero forzoso - eh-reh-DEH-roh for-SOH-soh - Compulsory heir
Albacea - ahl-bah-SEH-ah - Executor
Declaratoria de herederos - deh-klah-rah-TOH-ree-ah deh eh-reh-DEH-rohs - Declaration of heirs
Sucesión intestada - soo-seh-SYOHN een-tes-TAH-dah - Intestate succession
Desheredación - des-eh-reh-dah-SYOHN - Disinheritance
Mejora - meh-HOH-rah - Bequest (to a compulsory heir beyond their share)
Codicilo - koh-dee-SEE-loh - Codicil
Caucionar la herencia - kow-syoh-NAR lah eh-REN-see-ah - To secure the inheritance
Aceptación de la herencia - ah-sep-tah-SYOHN deh lah eh-REN-see-ah - Acceptance of the inheritance
Colación - koh-lah-SYOHN - Collation (of gifts)
Petición de herencia - peh-tee-SYOHN deh eh-REN-see-ah - Claim for inheritance

DIALOG

Según el testamento, a mí me corresponde la mitad de la herencia.
El codicilo posterior modifica eso y te otorga solo un tercio.
Presentaré una impugnación por indignidad ante el juzgado.
Tiene usted derecho a hacerlo, pero le recomiendo que reconsideremos la vía notarial.

English translation:
According to the will, I am entitled to half of the inheritance.
The subsequent codicil modifies that and grants you only a third.
I will file a challenge for unworthiness with the court.
You have the right to do so, but I recommend we reconsider the notarial route.

STORY

Tras el fallecimiento del causante, los herederos forzosos interpusieron una demanda de impugnación de testamento. Alegaban que el testamento ológrafo no cumplía con los requisitos legales de forma. El juez nombró un perito calígrafo para verificar la autenticidad de la firma y la fecha. El albacea suspendió la partición de la herencia hasta la sentencia definitiva.

English translation: After the death of the deceased, the compulsory heirs filed a will challenge lawsuit. They alleged that the holographic will did not meet the legal formal requirements. The judge appointed a handwriting expert to verify the authenticity of the signature and date. The executor suspended the division of the estate pending the final ruling.

BREACH OF CONTRACT TERMS

Incumplimiento de contrato - een-koom-plee-MYEN-toh deh kon-TRAH-toh - Breach of contract
Cláusula penal - KLAU-soo-lah peh-NAL - Penalty clause
Resolución - reh-so-loo-see-ON - Termination
Rescisión - reh-see-see-ON - Rescission
Daños y perjuicios - DA-nyos ee pehr-HWEE-see-os - Damages
Mora - MO-rah - Default
Cumplimiento forzoso - koom-plee-MYEN-toh for-SO-so - Specific performance
Fuerza mayor - FWEHR-sah mah-YOR - Force majeure
Buena fe - BWEH-nah FEH - Good faith
Dolo - DOH-loh - Fraud
Indemnización - een-dem-nee-sah-see-ON - Indemnity
Obligación contractual - oh-blee-gah-see-ON kon-trahk-TWAHL - Contractual obligation
Incumplimiento sustancial - een-koom-plee-MYEN-toh soo-stan-see-AHL - Material breach
Incumplimiento parcial - een-koom-plee-MYEN-toh par-see-AHL - Partial breach
Reclamación - reh-klah-mah-see-ON - Claim

DIALOG

El contrato establece claramente que el pago debía realizarse dentro de los treinta días naturales.
Usted incumplió el plazo de entrega, lo que constituye un incumplimiento sustancial de las condiciones pactadas.
Presenté una notificación por incumplimiento tal como exige la cláusula séptima.
Entonces procederé a interponer las acciones legales correspondientes por los daños y perjuicios causados.

English translation:
The contract clearly states that the payment was to be made within thirty calendar days.
You breached the delivery deadline, which constitutes a substantial breach of the agreed conditions.
I submitted a notice of breach as required by the seventh clause.
I will then proceed to file the corresponding legal actions for the damages caused.

STORY

La empresa incumplió las cláusulas esenciales del contrato de suministro. No entregó las mercancías en el plazo estipulado, lo que constituye un incumplimiento sustancial. La parte perjudicada ejerció su derecho a resolver el contrato y exigir la indemnización por daños y perjuicios conforme a lo establecido en el acuerdo y la ley aplicable.

English translation: The company breached the essential clauses of the supply contract. It failed to deliver the goods within the stipulated period, which constitutes a material breach. The aggrieved party exercised its right to terminate the contract and demand compensation for damages as established in the agreement and applicable law.

NON-DISCLOSURE AGREEMENTS

Confidencialidad - kohn-fee-den-see-ah-lee-DAHD - Confidentiality
Parte Reveladora - PAR-teh reh-beh-lah-DOH-rah - Disclosing Party
Parte Receptora - PAR-teh reh-sep-TOH-rah - Receiving Party
Información Confidencial - een-for-mah-see-ON kohn-fee-den-see-AHL - Confidential Information
Divulgación - dee-vool-gah-see-ON - Disclosure
Obligación de no divulgar - oh-blee-gah-see-ON deh no dee-vool-GAR - Obligation of non-disclosure
Propósito Limitado - pro-POH-see-toh lee-mee-TAH-doh - Limited Purpose
Duración - doo-rah-see-ON - Term
Jurisdicción - hoo-rees-deek-see-ON - Jurisdiction
Ley Aplicable - lay ah-plee-KAH-bleh - Governing Law
Remedio por Incumplimiento - reh-MEH-dyo por een-koom-plee-mee-EN-toh - Remedy for Breach
Daños y Perjuicios - DAH-nyos ee pehr-HWEE-see-os - Damages
Acuerdo - ah-KWER-doh - Agreement
Cláusula - KLAU-soo-lah - Clause
Firma - FEER-mah - Signature

DIALOG

¿Está listo para firmar el acuerdo de confidencialidad?
Sí, he revisado las cláusulas sobre la protección de la información sensible.
Perfecto. Recuerde que este contrato es vinculante y prohíbe la divulgación a terceros.
Entendido. Mantendré la confidencialidad de todos los datos según lo estipulado.

English translation:
Are you ready to sign the non-disclosure agreement?
Yes, I have reviewed the clauses regarding the protection of sensitive information.
Perfect. Remember that this contract is binding and prohibits disclosure to third parties.
Understood. I will maintain the confidentiality of all data as stipulated.

STORY

El abogado redactó un acuerdo de confidencialidad. El documento incluyó cláusulas sobre la protección de información privilegiada y secretos comerciales. La parte receptora aceptó las obligaciones de no divulgación. La vigencia del contrato se extendió más allá de la terminación del proyecto. Ambas partes firmaron el contrato, haciendo el acuerdo vinculante y ejecutable.

English translation: The lawyer drafted a non-disclosure agreement. The document included clauses on the protection of privileged information and trade secrets. The receiving party accepted the non-disclosure obligations. The contract's term extended beyond the project's termination. Both parties signed the contract, making the agreement binding and enforceable.

SERVICE CONTRACT EXPLANATIONS

Cláusula - KLAU-soo-lah - Clause
Obligaciones - oh-blee-gah-see-OH-nes - Obligations
Partes - PAR-tes - Parties
Duración - doo-rah-see-ON - Duration
Pago - PAH-goh - Payment
Incumplimiento - een-koom-plee-mee-EN-toh - Breach
Rescisión - reh-see-see-ON - Termination
Confidencialidad - kohn-fee-den-see-ah-lee-DAD - Confidentiality
Indemnización - een-dem-nee-sah-see-ON - Indemnity
Jurisdicción - hoo-rees-deek-see-ON - Jurisdiction
Garantía - gah-rahn-TEE-ah - Warranty
Cesión - seh-see-ON - Assignment
Fuerza Mayor - FWEHR-sah mah-YOR - Force Majeure
Acuerdo - ah-KWEHR-doh - Agreement
Anexo - ah-NEK-soh - Annex

DIALOG

El contrato de servicios establece las obligaciones y responsabilidades de cada parte.
Incluye cláusulas sobre confidencialidad, propiedad intelectual y el plazo de vigencia.
¿Qué sucede si una de las partes incumple sus obligaciones?
La parte afectada podría exigir el cumplimiento forzoso o reclamar una indemnización por daños y perjuicios.

English translation:
The service contract establishes the obligations and responsibilities of each party.
It includes clauses on confidentiality, intellectual property, and the term of validity.
What happens if one of the parties fails to meet its obligations?
The affected party could demand specific performance or claim compensation for damages.

STORY

El cliente celebró un contrato de servicios con el proveedor. El objeto del contrato era la consultoría legal. El incumplimiento de las obligaciones por una de las partes conlleva la resolución contractual. Ambas partes pactaron una cláusula penal por mora en la ejecución. El contrato se rige por la jurisdicción exclusiva de los tribunales de Madrid.

English translation: The client entered into a service contract with the provider. The contract's purpose was legal consultancy. Breach of obligations by one party leads to contract termination. Both parties agreed on a penalty clause for delay in performance. The contract is governed by the exclusive jurisdiction of the courts of Madrid.

TERMINATION CLAUSES

Despido - dess-PEE-doh - Dismissal
Despido improcedente - dess-PEE-doh eem-proh-seh-DEN-teh - Unfair Dismissal
Despido procedente - dess-PEE-doh proh-seh-DEN-teh - Fair Dismissal
Despido disciplinario - dess-PEE-doh dee-see-plee-nah-ree-oh - Disciplinary Dismissal
Indemnización - een-dem-nee-sah-see-ON - Severance Payment
Finiquito - fee-nee-KEE-toh - Settlement Agreement
Preaviso - preh-ah-VEE-soh - Notice Period
Causa justificada - KOW-sah hoos-tee-fee-KAH-dah - Just Cause
Incapacidad - een-kah-pah-see-DAHD - Incapacity
Dimisión - dee-mee-see-ON - Resignation
Mutuo acuerdo - MOO-too-oh ah-KWEHR-doh - Mutual Agreement
Periodo de prueba - peh-ree-OH-doh deh PROO-eh-bah - Probation Period
Cláusula resolutoria - KLOW-soo-lah reh-soh-loo-TOH-ree-ah - Termination Clause
Extinción del contrato - eks-teen-see-ON del kon-TRAH-toh - Termination of Contract
Liquidación - lee-kee-dah-see-ON - Final Pay Settlement

DIALOG

¿En qué casos puede rescindirse el contrato unilateralmente?
Por incumplimiento grave de las obligaciones pactadas.
¿Y qué sucede con los pagos pendientes?
El infedor deberá indemnizar los daños y perjuicios causados.

English translation:
In what cases can the contract be unilaterally terminated?
For a serious breach of the agreed obligations.
And what happens with pending payments?
The party in breach must compensate for the damages caused.

STORY

El contrato establece cláusulas de terminación por incumplimiento sustancial. La parte afectada notificará la mora, concediendo un plazo para remediarla. De no resolverse, se procederá a la resolución contractual. Las partes acuerdan indemnizaciones por daños y perjuicios, conforme a la legislación aplicable, liberándose de futuras obligaciones tras el cumplimiento de lo pactado en la cláusula.

English translation: The contract establishes termination clauses for substantial breach. The affected party will notify the default, granting a period to remedy it. If unresolved, contractual termination will proceed. The parties agree on compensation for damages, according to applicable law, releasing themselves from future obligations after compliance with the clause.

LIABILITY LIMITATIONS

Responsabilidad limitada - rohs-pohn-sah-bee-lee-DAHD lee-mee-TAH-dah - Limited liability
Exención de responsabilidad - ek-sen-see-ON deh rohs-pohn-sah-bee-lee-DAHD - Exemption from liability
Cláusula limitativa - KLAU-soo-lah lee-mee-tah-TEE-bah - Limitation clause
Límite de indemnización - LEE-mee-teh deh een-dem-nee-sah-see-ON - Limit of compensation
Fuerza mayor - FWEHR-sah mah-YOR - Force majeure
Negligencia - neh-glee-HEN-see-ah - Negligence
Culpa grave - KOOL-pah GRAH-beh - Gross negligence
Daños y perjuicios - DAH-nyos ee pehr-HWEE-see-os - Damages
Indemnización - een-dem-nee-sah-see-ON - Compensation
Acto de omisión - AHK-toh deh oh-mee-see-ON - Act of omission
Causa extraña - KAU-sah eks-TRAH-nyah - External cause
Vicio oculto - VEE-see-oh oh-KOOL-toh - Hidden defect
Caso fortuito - KAH-soh for-TWEE-toh - Fortuitous event
Riesgo inherente - ree-ES-goh een-eh-REN-teh - Inherent risk
Renuncia de garantías - reh-NOON-see-ah deh gah-rahn-TEE-ahs - Waiver of warranties

DIALOG

¿Hasta qué punto podemos limitar nuestra responsabilidad en este contrato?
Las cláusulas de limitación de responsabilidad no pueden cubrir daños por negligencia grave.
Entiendo. Entonces, ¿la indemnización máxima se limita al valor del contrato?
Exacto. Esa es la norma, salvo en los casos expresamente previstos por la ley.

English translation:
To what extent can we limit our liability in this contract?
Liability limitation clauses cannot cover damages for gross negligence.
I understand. So, the maximum compensation is limited to the value of the contract?
Exactly. That is the standard, except in cases expressly provided for by law.

STORY

El proveedor limitó su responsabilidad por daños indirectos en el contrato. El cliente sufrió lucro cesante pero la cláusula de exoneración era válida. Se verificó el cumplimiento de los requisitos de transparencia y la ausencia de dolo. La indemnización fue denegada conforme a los términos pactados y la normativa aplicable en materia de limitaciones de responsabilidad.

English translation: The provider limited its liability for indirect damages in the contract. The client suffered loss of profit but the exoneration clause was valid. Compliance with transparency requirements and the absence of fraud were verified. Compensation was denied according to the agreed terms and the applicable regulations on liability limitations.

BAD NEWS DELIVERY PHRASES

Lamentamos informarle - lah-men-TAH-mos een-for-MAHR-leh - We regret to inform you
Tenemos malas noticias - teh-NEH-mos MAH-las noh-TEE-syahs - We have bad news
Lo sentimos mucho - loh sen-TEE-mos MOO-choh - We are very sorry
El resultado no es favorable - el reh-sul-TAH-doh noh es fah-voh-RAH-bleh - The outcome is not favorable
El veredicto es desfavorable - el beh-reh-DEEK-toh es des-fah-voh-RAH-bleh - The verdict is unfavorable
La apelación fue denegada - lah ah-peh-lah-see-ON fweh deh-neh-GAH-dah - The appeal was denied
La solicitud ha sido rechazada - lah soh-lee-see-TOOD ah SEE-doh reh-chah-SAH-dah - The application has been rejected
Hemos perdido el caso - EH-mos pehr-DEE-doh el KAH-soh - We have lost the case
La sentencia es condenatoria - lah sen-TEN-syah es kon-deh-nah-TOH-ryah - The sentence is guilty
Su recurso fue desestimado - soo reh-KOOR-so fweh deh-ses-tee-MAH-doh - Your motion was overruled
No hay suficientes pruebas - noh eye soo-fee-see-EN-tes PRWEH-bahs - There is not enough evidence
Las pruebas eran insuficientes - las PRWEH-bahs EH-rahn een-soo-fee-see-EN-tes - The evidence was insufficient
El juez ha denegado la libertad condicional - el hoo-ETH ah deh-neh-GAH-doh lah lee-ber-TAHD kon-dee-see-oh-NAHL - The

judge has denied parole

Su petición de indulto fue rechazada - soo peh-tee-see-ON deh een-DOOL-toh fweh reh-chah-SAH-dah - Your petition for a pardon was rejected

El tribunal ha fallado en su contra - el tree-boo-NAHL ah fah-YAH-doh en soo KON-trah - The court has ruled against you

DIALOG

Lo siento, pero su apelación ha sido denegada.
¿Qué significa esto para mi caso?
Significa que la sentencia es definitiva y debe proceder al pago de la multa.
Entiendo. Gracias por la información.

English translation:
I'm sorry, but your appeal has been denied.
What does this mean for my case?
It means the sentence is final and you must proceed with the payment of the fine.
I understand. Thank you for the information.

STORY

El juez denegó la moción de apelación. La sentencia es firme y condenatoria. Se notifica al acusado de su derecho a interponer un recurso de revisión ante el tribunal superior. El plazo para ello es de cinco días hábiles. La ejecución de la pena procederá una vez agotadas todas las vías judiciales.

English translation: The judge denied the appeal motion. The sentence is final and convicting. The accused is notified of his right to file a review appeal with the higher court. The deadline for this is five business days. The execution of the sentence will proceed once all legal avenues are exhausted.

CASE UPDATE TERMINOLOGY

Audiencia - ow-dee-EN-see-ah - Hearing
Apelación - ah-peh-lah-see-ON - Appeal
Auto - OW-toh - Court Order
Causa - KOW-sah - Case, Lawsuit
Citación - see-tah-see-ON - Summons
Demanda - deh-MAN-dah - Complaint, Lawsuit
Dictamen - deek-TAH-men - Opinion, Report
Diligencia - dee-lee-HEN-see-ah - Proceeding, Formality
Escrito - es-KREE-toh - Pleading, Brief
Prueba - PRWEH-bah - Evidence
Recurso - reh-KOOR-soh - Motion, Appeal
Sentencia - sen-TEN-see-ah - Judgment, Sentence
Sobreseimiento - soh-breh-sey-ees-ee-MYEN-toh - Dismissal
Testigo - tes-TEE-goh - Witness
Veredicto - veh-reh-DEEK-toh - Verdict

DIALOG

¿Ya se ha presentado la demanda?
Sí, y el juzgado ya ha emitido el auto de admisión a trámite.
Perfecto. Entonces ahora esperamos la notificación para continuar.
Exacto. El siguiente paso será la audiencia previa.

English translation:
Has the lawsuit been filed yet?
Yes, and the court has already issued the order to admit the proceedings.
Perfect. Then now we wait for the notification to continue.
Exactly. The next step will be the preliminary hearing.

STORY

El juez denegó la moción de desestimación. La parte actora presentó nuevos medios de prueba. El tribunal citó a las partes para la vista oral. Se notificó la resolución al ministerio fiscal y a los procuradores. El procedimiento continúa su tramitación ordinaria.

English translation: The judge denied the motion to dismiss. The plaintiff submitted new evidence. The court summoned the parties for the oral hearing. The ruling was notified to the public prosecutor and the attorneys. The procedure continues its ordinary processing.

ENCOURAGING CLIENT PATIENCE

Entiendo - ehn-tee-EHN-doh - I understand
Aprecio su paciencia - ah-PREH-syoh soo pah-SYEN-syah - I appreciate your patience
Estamos trabajando en ello - ehs-TAH-mohs trah-bah-HAHN-doh ehn EH-yoh - We are working on it
Estos procesos toman tiempo - EHS-tohs proh-SEH-sohs TOH-mahn TYEHM-poh - These processes take time
Le mantendremos informado - leh mahn-tehn-DREH-mohs een-fohr-MAH-doh - We will keep you informed
Es un proceso necesario - ehs oon proh-SEH-soh neh-seh-SAH-ryoh - It is a necessary process
Gracias por esperar - GRAH-syahs pohr ehs-peh-RAHR - Thank you for waiting
Su caso es importante - soo KAH-soh ehs eem-pohr-TAHN-teh - Your case is important
Confíe en el proceso - kohn-FEE-eh ehn ehl proh-SEH-soh - Trust the process
Cada paso cuenta - KAH-dah PAH-soh KWEHN-tah - Every step counts
La justicia lleva su tiempo - lah hoos-TEE-syah YEH-vah soo TYEHM-poh - Justice takes its time
Estamos avanzando - ehs-TAH-mohs ah-bahn-SAHN-doh - We are making progress
Su tranquilidad es clave - soo trahn-kee-lee-DAHD ehs KLAH-veh - Your peace of mind is key
Pronto tendremos novedades - PROHN-toh tehn-DREH-mohs

noh-veh-DAH-dehs - We will have news soon
Valoramos su comprensión - vah-loh-RAH-mohs soo kohm-prehn-SYOHN - We value your understanding

DIALOG

Entiendo su preocupación, pero estos procesos legales requieren tiempo.
Cada documento debe revisarse con sumo cuidado para proteger sus intereses.
Sé que es frustrante, pero no podemos apresurar la justicia.
Tiene razón. Continuaré esperando, confiando en su profesionalismo.

English translation:
I understand your concern, but these legal processes take time.
Every document must be reviewed with great care to protect your interests.
I know it's frustrating, but we cannot rush justice.
You are right. I will continue waiting, trusting in your professionalism.

STORY

El abogado presentó la demanda. El proceso judicial requiere tiempo. El juez revisará las pruebas y los testigos declararán. Cada actuación procedimental sigue el plazo legal. La sentencia llegará tras la audiencia final. La paciencia es crucial en el sistema legal.

English translation: The lawyer filed the lawsuit. The judicial process requires time. The judge will review the evidence and the witnesses will testify. Each procedural action follows the legal deadline. The judgment will arrive after the final hearing. Patience is crucial in the legal system.

REQUESTING DOCUMENTATION

Solicito documentación - soh-lee-SEE-toh doh-koo-men-tah-see-ON - I request documentation
Por favor, envíe - por fah-BOR, en-BEE-eh - Please send
Necesito una copia - neh-seh-SEE-toh OO-nah KOH-pee-ah - I need a copy
Certificado de nacimiento - sehr-tee-fee-KAH-doh deh nah-see-mee-EN-toh - Birth certificate
Acta de matrimonio - AHK-tah deh mah-tree-MOH-nee-oh - Marriage certificate
Escritura pública - es-kree-TOO-rah POO-blee-kah - Public deed
Testamento - tes-tah-MEN-toh - Will
Poder notarial - poh-DEHR noh-tah-ree-AHL - Power of attorney
Contrato - kon-TRAH-toh - Contract
Sentencia judicial - sen-TEN-see-ah hoo-dee-see-AHL - Court ruling
Documento de identidad - doh-koo-MEN-toh deh ee-den-tee-DAHD - Identity document
Pasaporte - pah-sah-POR-teh - Passport
Factura - fak-TOO-rah - Invoice
Número de expediente - NOO-meh-roh deh eks-peh-dee-EN-teh - Case file number
Certificado de defunción - sehr-tee-fee-KAH-doh deh deh-foon-see-ON - Death certificate

DIALOG

¿Podría proporcionar el poder notarial actualizado, por favor?
Necesitaré también una copia del documento de identidad vigente.
Claro, aquí tiene ambos. ¿Requiere algo más adicionalmente?
Sí, por favor adjunte el escrito de demanda para revisión.

English translation:
Could you provide the updated power of attorney, please?
I will also need a copy of the current identification document.
Of course, here are both. Do you require anything else additionally?
Yes, please attach the statement of claim for review.

STORY

El abogado solicitó al juzgado la documentación del caso. Presentó un escrito formal requiriendo el expediente completo, las actas de las audiencias y las pruebas presentadas. La solicitud se fundamentó en el artículo 109 de la Ley de Enjuiciamiento Civil, ejerciendo el derecho de acceso a la información procesal para su cliente.

English translation: The lawyer requested the case documentation from the court. He filed a formal motion requiring the complete file, the hearing minutes, and the evidence presented. The request was based on article 109 of the Civil Procedure Law, exercising the right of access to procedural information for his client.

CLOSING A CASE EXPLANATIONS

Caso cerrado - KAH-so se-RAH-doh - Case closed
Archivar - ar-chee-VAR - To file away / To close (a case)
Resolución - reh-so-loo-see-ON - Resolution / Ruling
Sentencia firme - sen-TEN-see-ah FEER-meh - Final judgment
Recursos agotados - reh-KOOR-sos ah-go-TAH-dos - Remedies exhausted
No ha lugar - no ah loo-GAR - Dismissed / Unfounded
Absolución - ab-so-loo-see-ON - Acquittal
Sobreseimiento - so-breh-say-mee-EN-to - Dismissal (of a case)
Cosa juzgada - KO-sa hoo-GAH-dah - Res judicata
Ejecutoria - eh-heh-koo-TOH-ree-ah - Final and enforceable judgment
Conformidad - kon-for-mee-DAD - Agreement / Acceptance (of a ruling)
Desestimación - des-es-tee-mah-see-ON - Dismissal / Rejection (of a claim)
Conclusión del proceso - kon-kloo-see-ON del pro-SE-so - Conclusion of the proceedings
Fallo - FAH-yo - Verdict / Judgment
Auto de conclusión - OW-to de kon-kloo-see-ON - Order of closure

DIALOG

Hemos concluido la investigación y presentado el informe final al juzgado.
El tribunal ha revisado las pruebas y ha emitido el auto de sobreseimiento.
Por lo tanto, procedemos al archivo definitivo del caso.
De acuerdo. Notificaré a las partes sobre el cierre de las actuaciones.

English translation:
We have concluded the investigation and submitted the final report to the court.
The court has reviewed the evidence and has issued the dismissal order.
Therefore, we proceed with the definitive filing of the case.
Agreed. I will notify the parties about the closure of the proceedings.

STORY

El juez, tras examinar las pruebas y los alegatos de las partes, declara que no existen fundamentos para continuar. Se ordena el archivo definitivo del caso por falta de mérito. Se notifica la resolución de sobreseimiento a todos los involucrados, quedando el asunto concluido y firme.

English translation: The judge, after examining the evidence and the arguments of the parties, declares there are no grounds to continue. The definitive archiving of the case is ordered for lack of merit. The dismissal ruling is notified to all involved, the matter now concluded and final.

ADDRESSING THE JUDGE

Su Señoría - soo seh-NYOR-ee-ah - Your Honor
Señor Juez - seh-NYOR hoo-ETH - Mister Judge
Señora Jueza - seh-NYOR-ah hoo-EH-sah - Madam Judge
Vuestra Señoría - VOO-ehs-trah seh-NYOR-ee-ah - Your Lordship / Ladyship
El Juzgado - el hoo-THAH-doh - The Court
Su Magistrado - soo mah-hees-TRAH-doh - Your Magistracy
Su Despacho - soo des-PAH-choh - Your Chambers
Juez Presidente - hoo-ETH preh-see-DEN-teh - Presiding Judge
Señoría - seh-NYOR-ee-ah - Your Honor
A este Juzgado - ah ES-teh hoo-THAH-doh - To this Court
Ante el Tribunal - AN-teh el tree-boo-NAHL - Before the Court
Merced - mehr-THETH - Your Grace (archaic, formal)
Su Autoridad - soo ow-toh-ree-DAHD - Your Authority
La Corte - lah KOR-teh - The Court
Su Tribunal - soo tree-boo-NAHL - Your Tribunal

DIALOG

Señoría, solicito se admita la nueva prueba documental.
El tribunal la admite, proceda a fundamentar su pertinencia.
Esta prueba es esencial para acreditar el hecho controvertido.
Concedido. Presente los originales en el plazo de tres días.

English translation:
Your Honor, I request that the new documentary evidence be admitted.
The court admits it; proceed to argue its relevance.
This evidence is essential to prove the disputed fact.
Granted. Submit the originals within a period of three days.

STORY

Señoría, el acusado niega los cargos. La fiscalía presenta las pruebas periciales y el acta de incautación. Solicitamos la admisión de los documentos como prueba. El testigo declara bajo juramento. Basamos nuestra petición en el artículo 742 de la ley de enjuiciamiento criminal. Esperamos la resolución judicial.

English translation: Your Honor, the accused denies the charges. The prosecution presents the expert evidence and the seizure report. We request the admission of the documents as evidence. The witness testifies under oath. We base our petition on article 742 of the criminal procedure law. We await the judicial ruling.

JURY INSTRUCTIONS

Veredicto - veh-reh-DEEK-toh - Verdict
Deliberación - deh-lee-beh-rah-see-ON - Deliberation
Prueba - PRWEH-bah - Evidence
Testigo - tehs-TEE-goh - Witness
Carga de la prueba - KAR-gah deh lah PRWEH-bah - Burden of proof
Más allá de una duda razonable - mahs ah-YAH deh OO-nah DOO-dah rah-soh-NAH-bleh - Beyond a reasonable doubt
Declaración - deh-klah-rah-see-ON - Testimony
Hecho - EH-choh - Fact
Culpable - kool-PAH-bleh - Guilty
Inocente - ee-noh-SEN-teh - Not Guilty
Acusación - ah-koo-sah-see-ON - Prosecution
Defensa - deh-FEN-sah - Defense
Jurado - hwah-RAH-doh - Jury
Juez - HWETH - Judge
Testimonio - tehs-tee-MOH-nyoh - Testimony

DIALOG

Ustedes, como jurado, deben basar su veredicto únicamente en la evidencia presentada.
Entiendo. ¿Debemos considerar también las instrucciones legales que nos ha proporcionado?
Exactamente. Apliquen la ley que he explicado a los hechos que han escuchado.
Decidiremos el caso de manera imparcial y solo con lo visto en el juicio.

English translation:
You, as the jury, must base your verdict solely on the evidence presented.
I understand. Should we also consider the legal instructions you have provided us?
Exactly. Apply the law I have explained to the facts you have heard.
We will decide the case impartially and only with what was seen in the trial.

STORY

El demandante presentó una demanda por incumplimiento de contrato. Alegó que el demandado no ejecutó las obligaciones estipuladas en el acuerdo válido. Solicitó una indemnización por daños y perjuicios. El juez, tras evaluar la prueba pericial y los testimonios, encontró al demandado responsable. Se ordenó el pago de la indemnización y las costas procesales.

English translation: The plaintiff filed a lawsuit for breach of contract. He alleged that the defendant did not execute the obligations stipulated in the valid agreement. He requested compensation for damages. The judge, after evaluating the expert evidence and testimonies, found the defendant liable. Payment of compensation and court costs was ordered.

WITNESS EXAMINATION PHRASES

Su Señoría - soo sehn-YOH-ree-ah - Your Honor
¿Podría identificar al acusado? - poh-DREE-ah ee-dehn-tee-fee-KAHR ahl ah-koo-SAH-doh - Could you identify the defendant?
¿Dónde estaba usted? - DOHN-deh ehs-TAH-bah oos-TEHD - Where were you?
¿Qué sucedió entonces? - keh soo-seh-DYOH ehn-TON-sehs - What happened then?
¿Qué vio usted? - keh VEE-oh oos-TEHD - What did you see?
¿Está seguro/a? - ehs-TAH seh-GOO-roh/rah - Are you sure?
Objeción - ohb-hek-SYOHN - Objection
Sostengo la objeción - sohs-TEHN-goh lah ohb-hek-SYOHN - I sustain the objection
Retiro la pregunta - reh-TEE-roh lah preh-GOON-tah - I withdraw the question
¿Podría describir...? - poh-DREE-ah deh-skree-BEER - Could you describe...?
¿A qué distancia? - ah keh dees-TAHN-syah - From what distance?
¿Reconoce esta prueba? - reh-koh-NOH-seh EHS-tah PRWEH-bah - Do you recognize this evidence?
Le muestro el documento identificado como... - leh MWEHS-troh ehl doh-koo-MEN-toh ee-dehn-tee-fee-KAH-doh KOH-moh - I show you the document marked as...
¿Qué conversación escuchó? - keh kohn-behr-sah-SYOHN ehs-

koo-CHOH - What conversation did you hear?

¿Quién más estaba presente? - kyehn mahs ehs-TAH-bah preh-SEN-teh - Who else was present?

DIALOG

¿Puede identificar a la persona que cometió el delito?
Sí, puedo señalar al acusado en la sala.
¿Qué hizo exactamente esa persona?
Forzó la puerta y tomó el equipo electrónico.

English translation:
Can you identify the person who committed the crime?
Yes, I can point out the defendant in the room.
What exactly did that person do?
He forced the door and took the electronic equipment.

STORY

El testigo declaró bajo juramento. Relató los hechos ocurridos el día doce. Afirmó haber visto al acusado en el lugar. Su testimonio fue claro y consistente. La parte contraria procedió con el contrainterrogatorio. Cuestionó la credibilidad del testigo. El juez admitió la prueba testifical como evidencia. El secretario judicial levantó acta de la declaración.

English translation: The witness testified under oath. He recounted the events of the twelfth. He stated he had seen the accused at the location. His testimony was clear and consistent. The opposing party proceeded with cross-examination. They questioned the witness's credibility. The judge admitted the testimonial evidence. The court clerk recorded the statement.

OBJECTION TERMINOLOGY

Objeción - ob-hek-see-ON - Objection
Sustento - soos-TEN-toh - Grounds
Improcedente - eem-pro-seh-DEN-teh - Improper / Inadmissible
Funda - FOON-dah - To base / To found (a motion)
Improcedencia - eem-pro-seh-DEN-see-ah - Lack of legal basis
Inexistencia - in-ek-sis-TEN-see-ah - Non-existence
Incompetencia - in-kom-peh-TEN-see-ah - Lack of jurisdiction
Nulidad - noo-lee-DAHD - Nullity
Irrelevante - ee-reh-leh-VAN-teh - Irrelevant
Impertinente - eem-pehr-tee-NEN-teh - Impertinent / Not germane
Vicioso - vee-see-OH-soh - Defective / Vitiating
Vicio de forma - VEE-see-oh deh FOR-mah - Defect in form
Vicio de fondo - VEE-see-oh deh FON-doh - Defect in substance
Desestimar - des-es-tee-MAR - To overrule / To dismiss
Admitir - ad-mee-TEER - To admit / To allow

DIALOG

Su Señoría, presento una objeción por parte de la defensa.
La pregunta es inductiva.
Tiene razón. Retiro la pregunta.
La testigo puede proceder a contestar la pregunta reformulada.

English translation:
Your Honor, the defense presents an objection.
The question is leading.
You are right. I withdraw the question.
The witness may proceed to answer the rephrased question.

STORY

El abogado presentó una objeción por parte contraria durante el interrogatorio. Fundó su objeción en la pregunta capciosa y en la falta de fundamento fáctico. El tribunal sostuvo la objeción y amonestó al abogado que interrogaba. Se instruyó al jurado para que desestimara la pregunta improcedente del registro.

English translation: The lawyer raised an objection from the opposing party during the examination. He based his objection on the misleading question and lack of factual basis. The court sustained the objection and admonished the examining lawyer. The jury was instructed to disregard the improper question from the record.

CLOSING ARGUMENT PHRASES

En conclusión - en kon-klu-SYON - In conclusion
Por lo tanto - por loh TAN-toh - Therefore
Como resultado - KOH-moh reh-sul-TAH-doh - As a result
La evidencia muestra - lah eh-vee-DEN-syah MWEH-strah - The evidence shows
No hay duda - no eye DOO-dah - There is no doubt
Solicito una condena - soh-lee-SEE-toh OO-nah kon-DEH-nah - I request a conviction
Pido que se haga justicia - PEE-doh keh seh AH-gah hoos-TEE-syah - I ask that justice be done
Basándonos en los hechos - bah-SAN-doh-nos en lohs EH-chos - Based on the facts
Ustedes deben decidir - oos-TEH-des DEH-ben deh-see-DEER - You must decide
La culpa del acusado - lah KOOL-pah del ah-koo-SAH-doh - The defendant's guilt
Más allá de toda duda razonable - mas ah-YAH deh TOH-dah DOO-dah rah-soh-NAH-bleh - Beyond a reasonable doubt
El testimonio demuestra - el tes-tee-MOH-nyoh deh-MWEH-strah - The testimony demonstrates
En resumen de los hechos - en reh-SOO-men deh lohs EH-chos - In summary of the facts
Es claro que - es KLAH-roh keh - It is clear that
Pido que absuelvan a mi cliente - PEE-doh keh ahb-SWEL-vahn ah mee klee-EN-teh - I ask that you acquit my client

DIALOG

La evidencia presentada no deja lugar a dudas sobre la culpabilidad del acusado.
Por el contrario, mi cliente ha demostrado ser una persona íntegra y honesta.
Solicito al jurado que emita un veredicto de culpabilidad.
Pido a este tribunal que absuelva a mi cliente de todos los cargos.

English translation:
The evidence presented leaves no doubt about the defendant's guilt.
On the contrary, my client has proven to be a person of integrity and honesty.
I ask the jury to return a guilty verdict.
I ask this court to acquit my client of all charges.

STORY

El demandante presentó su demanda y pruebas. El testigo declaró bajo juramento. El perito presentó su dictamen. El acusado ejerció su derecho a la defensa. Las partes presentaron sus conclusiones. Tras analizar las pruebas y los fundamentos de derecho, se debe dictar sentencia de acuerdo con la ley.

English translation: The plaintiff filed his lawsuit and evidence. The witness testified under oath. The expert presented his report. The defendant exercised his right to defense. The parties presented their closing arguments. After analyzing the evidence and legal grounds, a verdict must be issued in accordance with the law.

AFFIDAVIT EXPLANATIONS

Declaración jurada - deh-klah-rah-see-ON hwah-RAH-dah - Sworn statement
Juramento - hoo-rah-MEN-toh - Oath
Notario público - noh-TAH-ree-oh POO-blee-koh - Notary public
Fiel traducción - fee-el trah-dook-see-ON - Faithful translation
Comparecer - kohm-pah-reh-SEHR - To appear before
Testigo - tehs-TEE-goh - Witness
Bajo pena de perjurio - BAH-hoh PEH-nah deh pehr-HOO-ree-oh - Under penalty of perjury
Diligencia - dee-lee-HEN-see-ah - Legal proceeding
Certificar - sehr-tee-fee-KAHR - To certify
Fecha de expedición - FEH-chah deh eks-peh-dee-see-ON - Date of issuance
Identificación - ee-den-tee-fee-kah-see-ON - Identification
Firma - FEER-mah - Signature
Sello notarial - SEH-yoh noh-tah-ree-AHL - Notarial seal
Datos personales - DAH-tohs pehr-soh-NAH-lehs - Personal data
Constancia - kohns-TAN-see-ah - Certification

DIALOG

¿Usted entiende que este documento es una declaración jurada?
Sí, entiendo que es un testimonio bajo juramento.
¿Jura decir la verdad completa ante la ley?
Sí, juro decir la verdad, so pena de perjurio.

English translation:
Do you understand that this document is an affidavit?
Yes, I understand it is testimony under oath.
Do you swear to tell the complete truth under the law?
Yes, I swear to tell the truth, under penalty of perjury.

STORY

El testigo presenció el accidente el 15 de octubre. Él proporcionó una declaración jurada detallando los hechos. El documento fue firmado ante notario público. La declaración describe la negligencia del conductor y la placa del vehículo involucrado. Esta prueba es crucial para la demanda por daños y perjuicios.

English translation: The witness observed the accident on October 15th. He provided an affidavit detailing the facts. The document was signed before a notary public. The statement describes the driver's negligence and the license plate of the vehicle involved. This evidence is crucial for the damages lawsuit.

SUBPOENA TERMINOLOGY

Citación - see-tah-see-OHN - Subpoena
Citación a testificar - see-tah-see-OHN ah tehs-tee-fee-KAHR - Subpoena to Testify
Citación de comparecencia - see-tah-see-OHN deh kom-pah-reh-SEN-see-ah - Subpoena to Appear
Orden de allanamiento - OR-den deh ah-yah-nah-mee-EN-toh - Search Warrant
Testigo - tehs-TEE-goh - Witness
Declaración - deh-klah-rah-see-OHN - Testimony
Deposición - deh-poh-see-see-OHN - Deposition
Prueba - PRWEH-bah - Evidence
Documento - doh-koo-MEN-toh - Document
Notificación - noh-tee-fee-kah-see-OHN - Service of Process
Oficial de la corte - oh-fee-see-AHL deh lah KOR-teh - Court Officer
Bajo juramento - BAH-hoh hoo-rah-MEN-toh - Under Oath
Desacato - deh-sah-KAH-toh - Contempt of Court
Querellante - keh-reh-YAN-teh - Complainant
Diligencia - dee-lee-HEN-see-ah - Legal Proceeding

DIALOG

¿Recibió la citación judicial que enviamos la semana pasada?
Sí, la recibí, pero no estoy seguro de entender los cargos.
La citación le ordena comparecer ante el tribunal como testigo.
Entiendo. ¿Debo llevar los documentos que solicitan?

English translation:
Did you receive the subpoena we sent last week?
Yes, I received it, but I'm not sure I understand the charges.
The subpoena orders you to appear before the court as a witness.
I understand. Should I bring the documents they requested?

STORY

El tribunal emitió un subpoena duces tecum ordenando al testigo presentar los documentos requeridos. El alguacil efectuó la notificación conforme a la ley. El destinatario debe acatar el mandamiento judicial dentro del plazo establecido. El incumplimiento puede resultar en sanciones por desacato.

English translation: The court issued a subpoena duces tecum ordering the witness to produce the required documents. The process server effected the notification in accordance with the law. The recipient must comply with the court order within the established period. Non-compliance may result in sanctions for contempt.

DEPOSITION PROCEDURES

Juramento - hoo-rah-MEN-toh - Oath
Declaración - deh-klah-rah-see-ON - Testimony
Testigo - tes-TEE-goh - Witness
Abogado - ah-boh-GAH-doh - Lawyer
Pregunta - preh-GOON-tah - Question
Respuesta - res-PWES-tah - Answer
Objeción - ob-hek-see-ON - Objection
Sustentar - soos-ten-TAR - To Sustain
Abogado de la parte contraria - ah-boh-GAH-doh deh lah PAR-teh kon-trah-REE-ah - Opposing Counsel
Testificar - tes-tee-fee-KAR - To Testify
Falso - FAHL-soh - False
Verdad - behr-DAHD - Truth
Exhibir - ek-see-BEER - To Exhibit
Documento - doh-koo-MEN-toh - Document
Conformidad - kon-for-mee-DAHD - Agreement

DIALOG

¿Jura usted decir la verdad?
Sí, juro decir la verdad.
¿Podría usted decir su nombre completo para que quede en el acta?
Mi nombre es María Guadalupe Reyes.

STORY

El testigo declaró bajo juramento. El abogado formuló objeciones durante el interrogatorio. La taquígrafa transcribió toda la declaración verbal. Las partes presentaron documentos como pruebas identificadas. Al finalizar, el testigo revisó y firmó la transcripción para certificar su veracidad. El notario certificó la legalidad del procedimiento.

English translation: The witness testified under oath. The lawyer stated objections during the examination. The court reporter transcribed the entire verbal testimony. The parties presented documents as identified exhibits. Upon finishing, the witness reviewed and signed the transcript to certify its veracity. The notary certified the legality of the procedure.

MOTION FILING TERMS

Moción - moh-SEEOHN - Motion
Escrito - ehs-KREE-toh - Brief
Solicitud - soh-lee-see-TOOD - Petition
Fundamentos - foon-dah-MEN-tohs - Grounds
Hechos - EH-chohs - Facts
Derecho - deh-REH-choh - Law
Juez - HOO-ehs - Judge
Tribunal - tree-boo-NAHL - Court
Parte - PAHR-teh - Party
Notificación - noh-tee-fee-kah-SEEOHN - Notification
Oposición - oh-poh-see-SEEOHN - Opposition
Resolución - reh-soh-loo-SEEOHN - Ruling
Apelación - ah-peh-lah-SEEOHN - Appeal
Auto - OW-toh - Court Order
Recurso - reh-KOOR-soh - Legal Remedy

DIALOG

¿Ya revisaste el escrito de la moción?
Sí, pero necesito adjuntar más pruebas documentales.
Entonces, debemos solicitar una prórroga para presentar.
De acuerdo, preparo el escrito de ampliación de plazo.

English translation:
Did you review the motion filing?
Yes, but I need to attach more documentary evidence.
Then, we must request an extension to file.
Agreed, I will prepare the extension request.

STORY

El demandante presentó una moción para desestimar la demanda por falta de jurisdicción. El tribunal evaluó los argumentos y las pruebas presentadas. Con base en los fundamentos de derecho, el juez denegó la moción. La orden judicial fue emitida, y el caso procedió a la fase de descubrimiento de pruebas.

English translation: The plaintiff filed a motion to dismiss the lawsuit for lack of jurisdiction. The court evaluated the arguments and evidence presented. Based on the legal grounds, the judge denied the motion. The court order was issued, and the case proceeded to the discovery phase.

APPEAL PAPERWORK VOCABULARY

Apelación - ah-peh-lah-see-OHN - Appeal
Recurso - reh-KOOR-so - Appeal / Legal remedy
Demandante - deh-mahn-DAHN-teh - Plaintiff / Petitioner
Demandado - deh-mahn-DAH-doh - Defendant / Respondent
Tribunal - tree-boo-NAHL - Court
Sentencia - sen-TEN-see-ah - Judgment / Sentence
Auto - OW-toh - Court Order
Recurrente - reh-koo-RREN-teh - Appellant
Recurrido - reh-koo-RREE-doh - Appellee
Fundamentos de Derecho - foon-dah-MEN-tos deh deh-REH-cho - Legal Grounds
Prueba - PRWEH-bah - Evidence
Alegatos - ah-leh-GAH-tos - Arguments / Pleadings
Notificación - noh-tee-fee-kah-see-OHN - Notification / Service of process
Juez - HWEHS - Judge
Secretario Judicial - seh-kreh-TAH-ree-oh hoo-dee-see-AHL - Clerk of the Court

DIALOG

¿Ha presentado ya el escrito de apelación?
Sí, pero necesito adjuntar el acta de la sentencia.
¿Incluyó los fundamentos de derecho?
Claro, y también la certificación de la sentencia.

English translation:
Have you already filed the appeal brief?
Yes, but I need to attach the court's judgment record.
Did you include the legal grounds?
Of course, and the certification of the judgment as well.

STORY

El recurrente interpuso un recurso de apelación ante el tribunal superior. Alegó error en la aplicación de la ley por el tribunal a quo. Solicitó la revocación de la sentencia y la absolución. El ministerio fiscal presentó sus alegatos oponiéndose. El tribunal admite a trámite el recurso y notifica a las partes para la vista.

English translation: The appellant filed an appeal with the higher court. He alleged an error in the application of the law by the lower court. He requested the revocation of the sentence and an acquittal. The public prosecutor presented arguments opposing it. The court admits the appeal for processing and notifies the parties for the hearing.

www.ingramcontent.com/pod-product-compliance
Lightning Source LLC
Chambersburg PA
CBHW050902160426
43194CB00011B/2253